Prague

A PHOTOGRAPHIC GUIDE TO PRAGUE

ARTFOTO

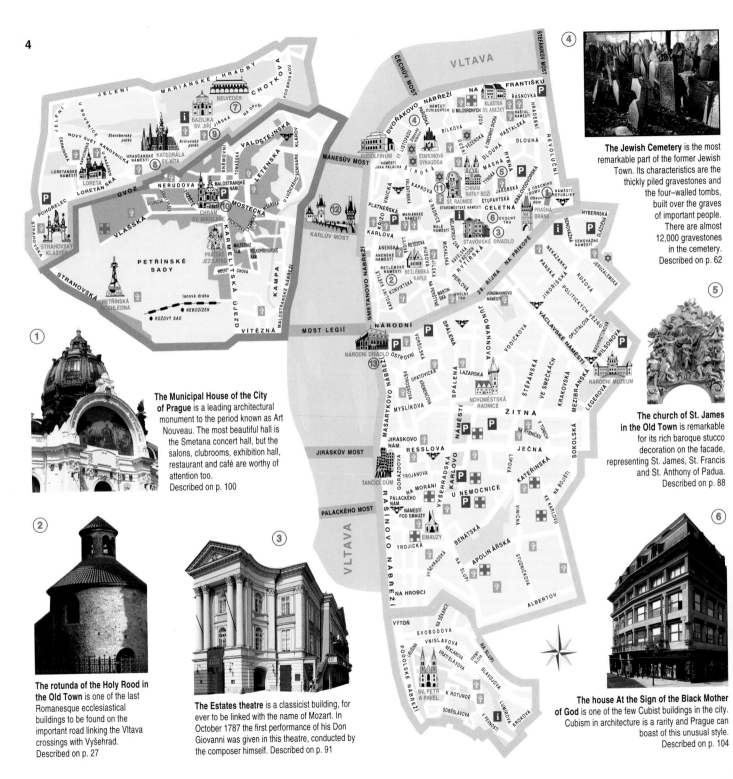

The Jewish Cemetery is the most remarkable part of the former Jewish Town. Its characteristics are the thickly piled gravestones and the four–walled tombs, built over the graves of important people. There are almost 12,000 gravestones in the cemetery. Described on p. 62

The Municipal House of the City of Prague is a leading architectural monument to the period known as Art Nouveau. The most beautiful hall is the Smetana concert hall, but the salons, clubrooms, exhibition hall, restaurant and café are worthy of attention too. Described on p. 100

The church of St. James in the Old Town is remarkable for its rich baroque stucco decoration on the facade, representing St. James, St. Francis and St. Anthony of Padua. Described on p. 88

The rotunda of the Holy Rood in the Old Town is one of the last Romanesque ecclesiastical buildings to be found on the important road linking the Vltava crossings with Vyšehrad. Described on p. 27

The Estates theatre is a classicist building, for ever to be linked with the name of Mozart. In October 1787 the first performance of his Don Giovanni was given in this theatre, conducted by the composer himself. Described on p. 91

The house At the Sign of the Black Mother of God is one of the few Cubist buildings in the city. Cubism in architecture is a rarity and Prague can boast of this unusual style. Described on p. 104

PRAGUE – the city of artistic styles

The Royal Summer Palace is said to be the most beautiful Renaissance building north of the Alps. Its arcades are decorated with reliefs on subjects from mythology and history, but also hunting and genre scenes. Described on p. 54

The basilica of St. George in Prague Castle is the second biggest church in Prague Castle. Its Romanesque origin (it was founded around 920) is shown by the remains of Romanesque paintings on the choir walls. Described on p. 23, 24

The Town Hall Horologe was made in 1410 by the clockmaker Mikuláš of Kadaň and the astronomer Jan Šindel. In 1490 this "miraculous machine" was repaired by Master Hanuš of Růže. Described on p. 39

The Charles Bridge is an indivisible part of the city panorama. Built during the reign of Charles IV., it is Gothic, but the statues decorating it come only from the 17th century. Described on p. 36, 80, 81

The cathedral of St. Vitus in Prague Castle is a Gothic architectural gem not only of Prague but of the whole country. The history of the cathedral is basically the history of the nation. Described on p. 29, 30, 31

The church of St. Nicholas in the Little Quarter the work of Christopher and Kilián Ignatius Dientzenhofer is one of the most important baroque buildings in Prague. The church contains a valuable organ dating from the middle of the 18th century on which Mozart himself played. Described on p. 76

The National Theatre a beautiful neo–Renaissance building, completed in 1883, is a treasurehouse of Czech 19th century art. Described on p. 96, 97

< St. John of Nepomuk

welcomes kindly all those who find their way to the New World – that strange part of Prague. Nowadays the New World is part of Hradčany, but in the 16th century the houses built here were on the fringe of the town. As you walk along the street you feel as if you were in the country – its so quiet and still here, and there's even a timbered country cottage. This romantic corner, formed of narrow streets and pretty little houses, makes an interesting contrast to the imposing buildings that tower above them – the Černín Palace and the Loretto church. The genius loci here has always attracted people with artistic souls, and it still does. For instance the famous violinist, František Ondříček, was born here, the composer Rudolf Friml lived here, and so did the Danish astronomer, Tycho de Brahe, for some time around 1600.

The Old Castle Steps

take you up from Klárov to the eastern gate of Prague Castle. There you come to one of the oldest towers of the original castle fortifications – the Black Tower. But before going through the gate to Jirská Street, you might like to stop at the little open space in front of the gate, as there is a wide view of the city from there. But this was not always such a pleasant place, at one time it was an execution ground. Noblemen who were condemned in the castle were executed outside its fortifications. Perhaps that is why there is a statue there of St. Barbora – the patron saint of the dying.
A more optimistic view of the past tells that there were vineyards on the surrounding slopes where Prince Wenceslas himself worked – later to become St. Wenceslas, patron saint of the Czech Lands.

A view of the Square of the Knights of the Cross, with a statue of Charles IV., the Old Town Bridge Tower and the Charles Bridge

The Square of the Knights of the Cross is said to be one of the most beautiful squares in Europe. Certainly it is true that in a small space you are surrounded by architectural treasures of various styles and dates. The Old Town Bridge Tower, standing on the first pillar of the Charles Bridge, is the pride of Gothic building and sculpture. The church of St. Francis has the reputation of being the most harmonious baroque church in Prague. Just opposite the Bridge Tower is the church of St. Saviour, whose wealth of figural decoration on the balustrade seems to inaugurate the ceremonial march of saints that continues across Charles Bridge.

In the middle of the square stands a bronze statue of Charles IV. a monarch who loved Prague above all other towns and assured her undying fame. There are many buildings in Prague marked by the spirit of Charles IV., but the three main ones can be called to mind in the immediate vicinity of his statue: the Charles Bridge, which is nearest, the St. Vitus' cathedral, visible across the river, and the Charles University, of which this statue holds the foundation charter in his right hand.

Hradčany Square

– view of the lst courtyard – the court of honour of Prague Castle. The main entrance to the grounds of Prague Castle is from Hradčany Square. From there hundreds of tourists stream into the castle, from there all official delegations enter the castle. But in times long past entry to the castle was not so easy as it is today. As the castle had no natural protection from this side, this was afforded by three deep and wide moats with drawbridges across them. When the castle was rebuilt in 1757, during the reign of Maria Theresa, the moats were levelled, giving rise to the present square in front of the main gateway.

The main gateway – decorated with figures of the Giants (by Ignác Platzer) – takes you into the lst courtyard of Prague Castle, and introduces you to its thousand years of history.

11

Prague – the city in the very heart of Europe – is a city that has not only a delightful position, a famous history, an amazing quantity of cultural monuments of all periods and styles, an interesting present and all the attractions of a metropolis, but something more in addition to all that. It has the inimitable atmosphere of a magical city, wreathed in strange stories that address the sensitive pilgrim at the most unexpected moments of his wanderings. Someone once said: "mystery is an abyss whose terrible depths entice our restless curiosity".

I should like – if you will allow me – to draw aside the veil of mystery a little, to satisfy your curiosity for a moment and initiate you into some of the stories.

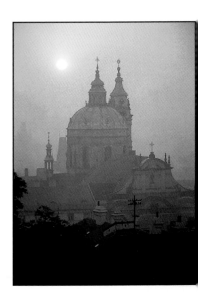

The longest story begins on the best known road, where your steps too will lead, the road of the Bohemian kings. This was the road taken by the coronation procession to the highest of honours. This procession entered the territory of the Old Town by what is now known as the Powder Tower (in the Middle Ages it was called the New Tower). It deserves observation, for it is majestic, well aware of its own value – for how many joys, hopes and maybe pain and disappointment too it has seen as it looked down on the magnificent processions that passed through it on their way to the castle. The state function of the tower was multiplied by a permanent link – a covered gallery leading directly to the Royal Court. For almost a century the Royal Court was the seat of the Bohemian kings. But when the seat in Prague Castle was improved the Royal Court became dilapidated and the tower gradually lost its state function. Today all that has remained of the Royal Court is a memorial tablet at the corner, but a link with the "stone beauty" of the tower still remains, for its neighbour is a very special house. The Municipal House of the capital city of Prague is one of the most imposing buildings in the Art Nouveau style from the beginning of the twentieth century. And it almost seems to have made the proud tower younger. Well, a neighbour several centuries younger does wonders. And very well they look together.

But to continue on the Royal Road. It leads through Celetná Street to the Old Town Square, to the pride of the Old Town burghers – the Town Hall. The longing of the Old Town aldermen – to have their own Town Hall, symbol of the city`s prestige – was only fulfilled in 1338, when King John of Luxemburg granted the right to set up a Town Hall. Delighted by the royal decision, they determined to have a very special Town Hall, its tower boasting an astronomical clock or horologe, something unique at that time. And since the 15th century this horologe mercilessly measures time for all passers-by, whether their heads be exalted or just ordinary. From the Town Hall the Royal Road crosses the Little Ring (now Little Square) to Charles Street and the Square of the Knights of the Cross. This square is worth a pause, as it is said to be one of the most beautiful in Europe. Its amazing what a friendly community is formed by the most different architectural styles existing beside one another, and how well they harmonize. In the middle of the square is a statue of "the father of the country" – Charles IV. Monumental buildings look down from all sides, and what a number of statues there are! Gazing from the Old Town Bridge Tower there is "the father of the country" again. Remember him, for you will find him present throughout Prague. If you walk under the tower you can appreciate the view of the Charles Bridge. During your stay in Prague you will probably cross it many times. It will draw you to it, as it has many visitors before you. For the Charles Bridge is an open-air art gallery that everyone can enter. The eloquent gestures of the statues of saints tell stories of love, devotion and faith. And as the bridge began, so it ends – with towers. If you pass through the Little Quarter towers you come to the territory of the Little Quarter, formerly known as the Lesser Town of Prague. Here the famous procession had to get its second wind, for the ascent that began in the Little Quarter Square and wound up along what is now Neruda Street to the Castle, was really not easy. You may imagine the coloured motley of that majestic procession, accompanied by peals of bells. But that is no dream, bells are still ringing in Prague. They ring with a melancholy note, or ponderous or even mischievous, as they did long ago, when they were the sound accompaniment to so great a scene.

     Have you not yet felt that touch of the magic city? Never mind – go on further, till you reach the spot where the royal procession came to an end and whither the steps of all visitors to our capital city wend – to Prague Castle. Catch your breath and look around. Before you spreads the splendid panorama of Prague, the city of a hundred spires. Not even the babel of languages can disturb the solemn feeling experienced when passing through the lofty baroque Matthias's Gate to places that are steeped in the history of the Czech nation. It is a good moment to think yourself centuries back into the past. For instance to the time of Charles IV. This outstanding man, diplomat and ruler loved Prague boundlessly. And he proved his love and persevering efforts to ensure his beloved city eternal glory by quite solid evidence: he had a beautiful stone bridge built, he founded the New Town of Prague, and in the grounds of the Castle – apart from his own seat – he had the impressive Gothic cathedral of St. Vitus erected. And those are only a few of the building works initiated by Charles IV.

     If you are able to slip into the St. Vitus cathedral in the early evening, when the crowd of tourists has thinned and the setting sun paints weird abstract patterns through the coloured mosaic of the windows, it will almost seem as if those spots of colour had taken on tangible form. Could it be that "the father of the country" had come himself with his train of courtiers to inspect the work of the master masons? If you are still slightly dazed by the magnificence of the cathedral, stay a little while more in times past and look at this architectural gem from the outside. Notice the richness of the Gothic system of buttresses. You see a city – turrets, indications of house gables, steps and railings. For the exterior of the cathedral was intended to represent God`s city. And the gargoyles are worth a glance-those imitations of monsters, devils and other evil beings. They are not mere decoration, nor the caprice of the builders. All the monsters have their significance. They protected the cathedral from being attacked by unclean spirits, for superstition says that if a demon sees his own image on the facade of a building, he takes fright and flies away.

And there was another emperor who was able to turn the attention of all the cultural cities of that day to his seat – Prague Castle. This was Rudolph II. Perhaps the greatest number of legends are entwined around this monarch. But a reality that he left behind him is the Spanish Hall in Prague Castle, which he had built to contain his collections – one of the richest renaissance collections of works of art and curiosities in the whole of Europe.

Prague is full of curiosities. One of them is Golden Lane. Once again, sadly, the truth is very sobre – it was the dwelling of the Castle gunners. But it is much more intriguing to believe – as the story tells – that it was the home of those who experimented and tempted fate, who promised His Imperial Majesty the philosophers' stone, the elixir of life and gold made from lead. That is one of the stories, but it is not a dream either. During the reign of Emperor Rudolph Prague was indeed full of charlatans and swindlers, but also of scientists and artists of great fame: Johannes Kepler, Tycho de Brahe, Adrien de Vries and many others. A medley of characters and nationalities. Magic hovers over the whole of this period and locality. And the magic of Rudolph's time will accompany you a little longer if you leave Golden Lane and the Black Tower, which is in fact white, leave the area of the Castle behind you, go down the Old Castle Steps to Klárov and maybe across the Mánes Bridge to the Old Town Square into the church of Our Lady Before Týn. There is the tomb of Rudolph's astronomer and favourite, Tycho de Brahe. And the Týn church itself is another pearl of Gothic art. And now one more worth-while turn off the path. A little way off the Old Town Square the Prague Jewish ghetto began. On the corner of Maisel Street, at the entrance to the ghetto, on house No. 5 there is a bust of Franz Kafka by the sculptor Karel Hladík from 1967. The mysterious name of Franz Kafka. There is hardly a visitor who does not want to see the place where Josef K. walked. The dominant of the former Jewish Town is the Old-New synagogue – the oldest preserved synagogue in Central Europe (1270–1280) and next to it is the Jewish Town Hall. If you look up to its gable you will see the clock with a Hebrew clockface, on which the hands go "backwards". It may take you back in time, to ancient days, when what you are looking at today originated.

And so our guide could go on enumerating places and buildings that deserve your attention, and where mystery and reality are so closely interwoven. But this book does not want to decide where you should go, only briefly to tell you of the wealth of our city and leave to you the choice of what you go and see. But so that our story should have some system, we have divided the Prague memorials into chapters according to their architectural style, and tried to show those you should not miss.

Prague grew up at the crossroads of the ancient trade routes. To find the beginnings of Prague the best way is to look at the history of Prague Castle in Hradčany.

Prague castle was founded in the second half of the 9th century by Prince Bořivoj of the tribe of the Czechs on a bare cliff promontory. Soon it became the permanent seat of later Přemyslide princes, who until then had lived and ruled in Levý Hradec. Even before the end of the 9th century Prague Castle was the centre of the growing Přemyslide state.

In 965 – 966 the Jewish Arab merchant Ibráhím ibn Jakub visited Prague and described it as a city built of stone and lime, and as a city with a busy trade. Even though the testimony of the merchant Ibráhím seems a bit enthusiastic on the basis of present knowledge based on archeological research, the seat of the Castle and the growing settlement below it certainly prospered well.

After 1085 extensive building activity continued in Vyšehrad under King Vratislav II. He was the first Bohemian king who held that title himself alone and he improved not only the castle site in Hradčany, but also that in Vyšehrad. That was where he founded the second Prague chapter, rebuilt the palace, founded and built three churches, of which the remains of the church of St. Lawrence and the rotunda of St. Martin are still preserved today.

Settlements grew up between the Vyšehrad and Hradčany castles and these were connected by a linking road. Further building sites dating from that time – the period known as Romanesque – are to be found on this road and at the two castle sites as well.

Hana Bílková

<< Wenceslas Square with the illuminated National Museum

Today Wenceslas Square is the main Prague artery, through which commercial and social life pulse day and night. It is named after the statue of St.Wenceslas, surrounded by the four patron saints of the country (by J. V. Myslbek) which stands at its head. In the Middle Ages the square was a marketplace and was called the Horse Market. It was one of three markets planned by Charles IV. when he founded the New Town of Prague.Originally both market and square were purely places of commerce. But as the centuries passed and social changes took place, the square became a kind of public tribunal, where people could express their satisfaction or the reverse. Many times has St. Wenceslas looked down on stormy demonstrations by the crowds. Those in which the nation strove for independence and protested against any kind of totalitarianism are unforgettable. And that is why, near the memorial to St. Wenceslas there is a symbolical memorial to all the victims of totalitarian regimes.

At the top of Wenceslas Square stands the National Museum, on the site where the St. Prokop or Horse Gate used to be.

The Charles Bridge, illuminated in the evening

The river Vltava divides the city, but a bridge links it together again. There are 18 bridges in Prague. The most beautiful, most romantic and the oldest is the Charles Bridge. The Charles Bridge is not only the pride of Gothic architecture, but an outdoor gallery that is open to everyone. The touching fates of the saints remind visitors of the stories of people who sacrificed earthly joys to their faith.

The unassuming originally Renaissance **Vrtba Palace**, standing on the corner of Karmelitská and Tržiště streets, hides one of the most charming and best-preserved palace gardens in Prague. The palace originated by connecting two houses (one of which belonged to Kryštof Harant of Polžice and Bezdružice – a Czech humanist scholar, who was executed in 1621 in the Old Town Square). After the Battle of the White Mountain both houses were confiscated. Jan Josef of Vrtba was responsible for rebuilding the houses and laying out the garden. He summoned the architect F. M. Kaňka, who planned the terraced garden on the site of a former vineyard in 1715 – 1720. He then invited the sculptor Matyáš Braun, who created the statues on the steps and terraces of classical gods, groups of putti and decorative vases. The salla terrena is decorated with frescos by V. V. Reiner (about 1721).

The Old Town Square with the memorial to John Huss and the baroque church of St. Nicholas

Every house and every stone in the Old Town Square has its history. There is mention of it as a market place on the right bank of the river Vltava from as early as around 1100. But even before then a large enclosed court, called Týn, was built next to the market where there was a customs house for foreign merchants – Ungelt. The duty collected benefitted not only the prince's treasury, but the Old Town merchants too. They started to build a little church (where the church of St. Nicholas now stands), a school and private houses. Then in the mid – 14th century the Old Town citizens gained the right to build their own Town Hall.

The Square has witnessed many dramatic events. Celebrations have taken place here, popular up-risings and executions. The cruellest of them – the execution of 27 Czech lords, leaders of the revolt of the Czech Estates against the Habsburg emperor and Bohemian king in 1621, was presented as a drama with a tragic end, and it meant a long period of stagnation in the development not only of the Square but of the whole city.

In the middle of the Square is the Art Nouveau memorial to Master John Huss (sculptor Ladislav Šaloun). Huss is surrounded by a group of Hussite warriors and people who became exiles after the Battle of the White Mountain. The memorial was unveiled on 6th July 1915, the five hundredth anniversary of the day John Huss was burnt at the stake in Constance.

The baroque dominant of the Square is the work of Kilián Ignác Dientzenhofer from 1732 – 1735 – the church of St. Nicholas.

For centuries the **Jewish Town Hall**, together with the **Old-New-Synagogue**, has been a symbol of the spiritual culture of Prague's Jewish Town.
The synagogue and the Town Hall used to be the vital centre of the religious community, the place where decisions were taken on common affairs, and the focal point of education and teaching. The Jewish Town Hall is and always has been a tourist attraction, especially because of the clock with a Hebrew clock-face and hands that go "backwards", built into the gable in 1765, which is also a favourite theme for writers and poets.

The Svatopluk Čech Bridge
is the first 20th century Prague bridge. It was built in 1906 – 1908 in Art Nouveau style from a design by architect Jan Koula, and has many cast iron and bronze statues. The four statues of Victory on cast iron columns on the stone toll houses are the work of Antonín Popp, and the Lantern–bearers on the upstream pillars are the work of Karel Opatrný and Ludvík Wurzel. The latter also designed the two six–headed hydras that guard the city coat–of–arms on the down–stream pillars. The railings are decorated on the outside with bands of metal relief medallions with a personification of Prague and wrought bronze panels with rams' heads.

Prague

ROMANESQUE

The definition of the various historical styles is most easily legible on architectural monuments. Works of the past are divided into artistic styles according to the external signs of the buildings, i.e. the portals, windows, arches, columns, ornaments and many other attributes. But you will find a building that is pure in style only exceptionally, because ancient monuments were rebuilt and enlarged by later generations and so in later styles.

The earliest style to be found in Prague monuments is Romanesque. This covers roughly the period from the 11th to the 13th centuries, and it is typically represented by the rotunda and the basilica, that is ecclesiastical buildings. Both these types of sacred building are marked by simplicity, small enclosed areas with narow little windows. The bigger double windows are divided by pillars. In the basilicas the ceilings were wooden, later round arches were used. There was usually a semi–circular relief tympanum over the entrance to the church.

Examples of monuments from this period are: Soběslav's hall in Prague Castle, St. George's basilica in Prague Castle, the Black Tower and part of the fortifications of Prague Castle, St. Martin's rotunda in Vyšehrad, the rotunda of the Holy Rood in the Old Town, the former one–storey house No. 156 in Huss street in the Old Town and the house of the Lords of Kunštát in Řetězová street No. 3 in the Old Town.

The Basilica of St. George in Prague Castle

(Prague 1 – Hradčany, U sv. Jiří Square)

is the second largest church in Prague Castle. Two slender, white granite towers of
unequal width shine over the panorama of Hradčany. The foundation stone of
the building, then still a rotunda, was laid around 920 by Prince Vratislav I. (the father
of St. Wenceslas). In 973 Mlada, the sister of Boleslav II., founded a convent next to
the church, and it was she who, having been ordained in Rome, brought the first
Benedictine nuns to Bohemia. It was Mlada too who was responsible for enlarging the
Romanesque rotunda into a basilica with a nave and two aisles. At the beginning of
the 13th century the late Romanesque chapel of St. Ludmila was added to
the southern tower. The southern portal of the basilica (from George Street) is
decorated with a relief showing St. George fighting the dragon (sculptor Benedikt
Ried). However the western facade is definitely baroque, having been built by
Francesco Caratti in 1671) and František Maxmilián Kaňka (in 1718 – 1722).
The statues on the facade are of Prince Vratislav and the Abbess Mlada.

View of the nave of St. George's basilica
The basilica has Romanesque compound triple windows and a crypt under the raised presbytery. The crypt dates from the 12th century and it used to contain the tomb of the Abbess. The basilica is the last resting place of several of the Přemyslide princes, among them its founder – Prince Vratislav (a stone tomb with a painted adjunct). There are still some remains of Romanesque paintings on the walls of the choir. In the southern wall of the church there is the chapel of St. Ludmila. It was Charles IV. who had her tombstone made, although the saint's body had been brought to the church in 925.

The Black Tower >>
together with the renaissance gateway, guards the entrance to the Castle from the east. Today this tower is the only preserved and visible one left of the Romanesque fortifications of Prague Castle, built during the reign of Soběslav I. Originally there was a gateway through it. Over the centuries the tower underwent many changes. For instance, during the reign of Charles IV. it had a wooden gallery with turrets at the corners and a gilded roof, so it was named Golden. In the 16th century it was a prison for debtors and ruffians. It gained the name Black after a fire in 1538 that blackened its walls. But even after it was cleaned and repaired its name was never changed.

Soběslav's Hall in the Royal Palace of Prague Castle

The Royal Palace took a long time to grow. Its foundations consist of the Romanesque palace of Prince Soběslav I., dating from the first half of the 12th century. In 1135, when Prince Soběslav decided to move his seat from Vyšehrad back to Prague Castle, he had it thoroughly rebuilt, changing what had been the Přemyslides' castle home into a real medieval fortress. This Romanesque rebuilding was so thorough that for the rest of the 12th and practically the whole of the 13th century no further changes were needed.

New fortifications were made of granite, and a new palace set up, 50 metres long and 10 metres wide, containing a hall with rolled vaulting (in the picture), a chamber for the princes to live in and a chapel dedicated to All Saints.

House No. 156 in Husova Street
(Prague 1 – Staré Město)
proudly displaying Venetian-type renaissance gables – it hides underground a beautiful Romanesque hall with four fields of crossed arches rising from a central column. This hall was once part of a Romanesque farmstead, built in the 12th century. Today the whole house is used for exhibitions.

The house of the Lords of Kunštát and Poděbrady
(Prague 1 – Staré Město, Řetězová ulice (Chain Street) No. 3) is a remarkable memorial to the architecture and culture of the Romanesque period (2nd half of the 12th century). The palace was a dwelling built within a farmstead. In the cellar (which used to be the ground floor) there are three vaulted rooms, of which the middle one has six fields of crossed arches resting on two mighty columns. We do not know the name of the builder, but the name of the owners. The first well-known owner was the supreme provincial scribe Boček of Kunštát, and the most famous was the Bohemian king, George of Poděbrady, who reigned from 1458 – 1471.

Rotundas are the oldest type of church buildings.

The chapel of the Holy Rood (Prague 1 – Staré Město, Karolina Světlá Street)
was built by an important road from Vyšehrad to the fords across the Vltava.
It dates from about the second quarter of the 12th century. In the nave there are
still the remains of Gothic paintings from the 14th century (The Coronation of the
Virgin Mary). The rotunda is surrounded by a neo-Romanesque lattice, made from
a design by the Czech painter Josef Mánes.

The Rotunda of St. Martin (Prague 2 – Nové Město, Vyšehrad)
This rotunda was probably once a parish church founded by Prince
Vratislav II. in the 2nd half of the 11th century, when he intended to make Vyšehrad
the new centre of the Přemyslides. It is the only building from the early Middle
Ages to be preserved in this locality. The walls are the original ones, but the main
portal is pseudo-Romanesque.

Prague
GOTHIC

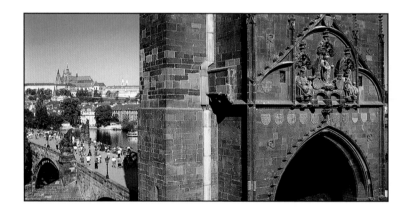

The Romanesque style was followed by the Gothic style, which came to the Czech Lands in the second quarter of the 13th century. In the country of its origin – France – it is called style ogival – the refracted style. The name itself tells of one of the characteristic signs of this style.

The most typical representatives of the Gothic style are again ecclesiastical buildings – cathedrals. Pointed arches, ribbed vaulting, a large number of external buttresses, and everywhere verticality, emphasizing the upward direction – those are the signs of the new style. The ribbed vaulting and buttress system enable the dematerialization of the walls, which are filled with an ever increasing number of windows. The architecture is abundantly decorated with sculptural details with figural, animal and plant themes. Both the external and internal walls, not to mention the ceiling beams, ribbing and frames are brightly painted, so that Gothic buildings were almost more colourful than we are able to imagine today. There was a great deal of building activity during the Gothic period, and not only ecclesiastical buildings were put up, but secular ones, such as rich burghers' houses, town halls, bridges and city fortifications.

The Gothic style put down deep roots in this country and from the beginning of the 14th century it strongly marked the face of the towns. Between the years 1310 and 1419 Prague became the biggest city in Europe, and this was the time when the most beautiful Gothic buildings originated there. This period is called the time of Czech Gothic. The most beautiful Prague Gothic memorials include: the cathedral of St. Vitus, the Vladislav hall in Prague Castle (late Gothic), the church of Our Lady under the Chain in the Little Quarter, the Charles Bridge, the Old Town Bridge Tower, the Town Hall of the Old Town, the church of Our Lady Before Týn, the house At the Sign of the Stone Bell in the Old Town Square, the Carolinum, the Powder Tower, the St. Agnes convent, the Old–New synagogue, the Maisel synagogue, the church of Our Lady of the Snows in Jungmann Square, the Bethlehem chapel, the monastery na Slovanech (Emmaus) with the church of the Virgin Mary, St. Jerome and the Slav patron saints.

The southern facade of the St. Vitus cathedral with the Golden Gate (Prague – Prague Castle)

The St. Vitus cathedral is not only the main church in the Castle, but a spiritual centre and architectural gem of the whole nation. The Golden Gate – once the main entrance to the cathedral – is separated from the nave by a hallway – part of the cathedral most decorated by the stonemasons. The mosaic on the front of the Golden Gate is most precious, it represents the Last Judgment: Christ is in the middle, below him kneel the patron saints of the country and lower still, at the sides, Charles IV. and his wife Eliška of Pomerania.

The mosaic was made in 1370–1371 from a design by Italian masters of split quartz and glass in 33 shades of colour.

The cathedral spire – the unfinished work of Petr Parléř – is 96.5 metres high and is topped by a renaissance helmet supporting a gilded Czech lion 3.5 metres high. There are 4 bells in the tower: the one named Zikmund, founded by Tomáš Jaroš in 1549, is the biggest bell in Bohemia.

The western facade of the cathedral > is neo-Gothic, with two spires 82 metres high (architects Josef Mocker and Kamil Hilbert). The rose window illustrates the various days of the Creation of the World (designed by František Kysela in 1921). The bronze doors of the cathedral portray the history of its building.

The window in the **New Archbishop's chapel**, with scenes from the life of the apostles SS. Cyril and Methodius, was made from a picture by the Czech painter Alfons Mucha – 1931.

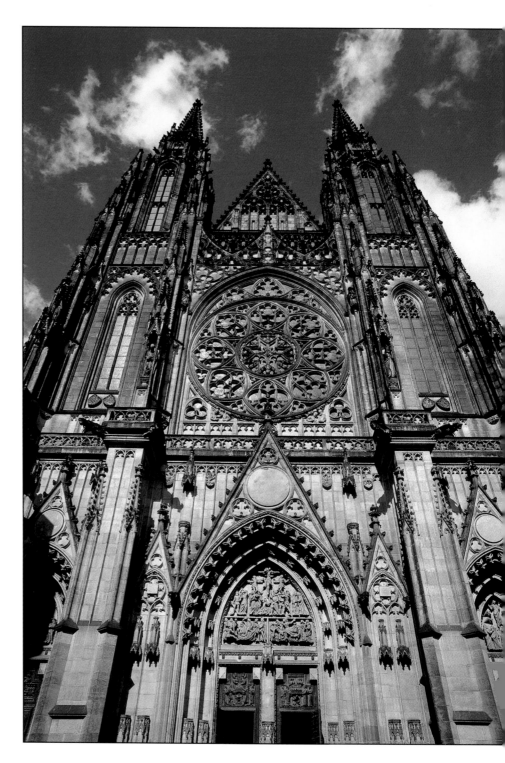

The Interior of the St. Vitus Cathedral

The original Romanesque rotunda of St. Vitus was founded in the twenties of the 10th century by Prince Wenceslas. It was built at the highest point of Prague Castle and the relics of St. Vitus were preserved in it. Prince Spytihněv had the rotunda torn down and in its place he began to build a basilica, which was completed by his successor, Vratislav II. (1096). When the Prague bishopric was promoted to an archbishopric in 1344 the representatives of ecclesiastical and temporal power decided to build a new church. And so in that year the foundation stone for a Gothic cathedral was laid by John of Luxemburg and his sons, Karel and Jan Jindřich. The first builder in 1344 – 1352 was Matthias of Arras, who built eight chapels in the east end of the cathedral. After his death the work was taken over by 23-year-old Petr Parléř. During his lifetime he managed to build the remainder of the choir chapels, the triforium and the vault of the choir. He also began to build the transept and the tower.

The cathedral is 124 metres long, 60 metres wide across the transept and the main arch is 33 metres high. The vault over the nave is reticulated and Petr Parléř was the first in Central Europe to use this type of vaulting.

<< Portraits of Charles IV. and Petr Parléř in the St. Vitus triforium
The triforium is a unique portrait gallery of stone busts. This was set up in around 1380 and contains 11 busts of members of the imperial family, 3 of Prague archbishops, 5 of men who directed the building of the cathedral and those of the two builders, Matthias of Arras and Petr Parléř. In the modern part of the church the gallery has been completed with busts of the artists deserving of merit for finishing the building.

The St. Wenceslas Chapel in the St. Vitus Cathedral
is the most precious place in the cathedral, for it is where the relics of St. Wenceslas – patron saint of the Czech Lands – are kept. It was built in 1344 – 1364 and arching over it is Parléř's vault of stars. The decoration of the chapel is an example of the high standard of Bohemian art in the 14th century. The lower part of the walls is inlaid with semi-precious stones and among them pictures of Christ's passion by an unknown painter from 1372 – 1373. Above these is a second cycle of pictures on all the walls, with scenes from the life of St. Wenceslas. These are the work of the Master of the Litoměřice altar from 1506 – 1509. Portraits of the four Czech patron saints are composed into this cycle over the altar. In the centre stands a beautiful statue of St. Wenceslas by Jindřich Parléř (Petr Parléř's nephew) from 1373. Over the St. Wenceslas chapel is the coronation chamber, where the Bohemian crown jewels are kept.
The iron door in the chapel's northern portal, cast in the 2nd half of the 14th century, is inset with a Romanesque bronze ring. Tradition tells that this is the ring handle of the door of the church of SS. Kosmas and Damian in Stará Boleslav, which St. Wenceslas caught hold of when assaulted by his murderers.

The Vladislav Hall of the Old Palace in Prague Castle

is the largest secular room of medieval Prague. It was built during the reign of King Vladislav of the Jagellons in 1493 – 1502 from plans by the architect Benedikt Ried. It is 62 metres long, 16 metres wide and 13 metres high. The late Gothic stellar vaulting is remarkable. The outside of the windows is now in renaissance style. The hall was used for banquets and royal audiences, not only coronation feasts and balls were held there, but knightly tournaments on horseback.
It was the site of markets where antique dealers sold their goods. Since 1918 it has been the scene of important state occasions, for instance the election of the president.

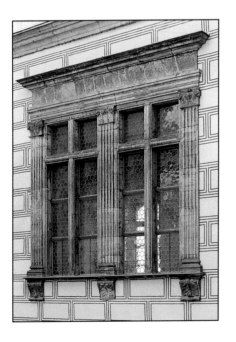

The church of the Virgin Mary under the Chain

(Prague 1 – Malá Strana, Lázeňská Street) was originally
a Romanesque church belonging to the Order of the Knights of St. John
(Johannites), later to the Knights of Malta. The church and the
monastery were founded in 1159 by King Vladislav II., who came to
know the knights on a crusade in Palestine. During the reign of Charles
IV. it was rebuilt in Gothic style by the Parléř building works, which made
it into an imposing edifice with a nave and 2 aisles with apses and two
towers in the facade. When the whole of the Little Quarter was engulfed
by fire in 1420 both church and monastery were destroyed. In 1519 the
presbytery was renewed and the damaged tower was lowered. But the
church remained unfinished. Behind the great Gothic towers and
antechamber there is no nave but a long garden with the present church
at the end of it – basically the Gothic presbytery of the intended church.
Over the main altar is a picture by Karel Škréta of the Virgin Mary and
St. John the Baptist helping the Knights of Malta in their victorious naval
battle against the Turks in 1571. The Knights of Malta were knighted
under this picture.

The Charles Bridge

known as the pearl of the medieval art of building. It has borne the name of its founder only since 1870. Before then it was called simply the Stone or Prague Bridge. Like many other Gothic buildings the Charles Bridge had its predecessor – the stone Judith Bridge (Judith was the wife of King Vladislav I.). But the Judith Bridge was narrower and it had many strong wide pillars, yet in 1342 it was swept away by a mighty flood. So on 9th July 1357 Charles IV. laid the foundation stone of the present bridge
on the Old Town side. The building was entrusted to Petr Parléř and it continued from 1357 till the beginning of the 15th century. The bridge is 520 metres long and 9.5 metres wide, the 16 arches rest on 2 pillars on the banks, 12 in the water and 3 on Kampa Island. The bridge was paved from its very beginnings. It turns and slopes down towards the Little Quarter, opening up new views of the panorama.
At first the bridge was decorated with a simple cross, the statues only having been there since the 17th century.

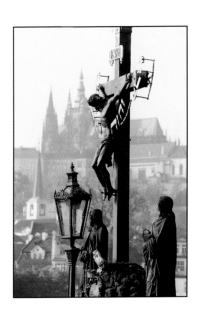

There are towers with gateways at both ends of the bridge, making it a kind of fortress. There are two towers at the Little Quarter end, one at the Old Town end.

The Little Quarter towers stand on either side of a Gothic gateway.

On the gate's toothed battlements are the Czech, German and Upper Lusatian coats of arms, beneath them those of the Old Town and the Little Quarter. The lower Little Quarter tower, built before 1135, is originally Romanesque and is the remains of the fortifications of a settlement on the left bank of the Vltava, so it is still older than the Judith Bridge. After 1591 it was restored in renaissance style. The taller Little Quarter Tower was built in 1464 during the reign of King George of Poděbrady and was intended as an imitation of Parléř's model at the opposite end of the bridge. It was repaired in the 19th century.

The Old Town Bridge Tower

has the reputation of being the most beautiful tower of its kind in Europe. It was built in 1380 by the builder of the St. Vitus cathedral Petr Parléř and his works, though the decoration of the tower was added to later. There is a wealth of decoration on the eastern face. The Gothic arch of the gateway has 28 rosettes round it. Over the arch are the coats of arms of the countries ruled by the Luxemburgs. At the first floor level are statues of the seated kings Charles IV. and Wenceslas IV., and between them stands the patron saint of the bridge, St. Vitus, who is also the patron saint of the Roman Empire and the Kingdom of Bohemia. The statues are good examples of the work of Gothic sculptors from 1380. At the second floor level, under the battlements with a passageway are the windows and statues of the Czech patron saints – St. Adalbert and St. Zikmund – in niches. All around the statues of rulers and saints there are kingfishers. The kingfisher was the favourite emblem of Wenceslas IV., but it was also the emblem of bathkeepers, and this gave rise to the legend about Zuzana the bathkeeper, who saved the king's life. There used to be a gate in the gateway that, like other gates in fortresses, was closed with a grating, to be let down when danger threatened. That was the case in February 1611, when Prague was attacked by soldiers from Passau. When they had plundered the Little Quarter they stormed the bridge so as to continue their looting in the Old Town. But they were welcomed by a closed grating with the people of Prague shooting through it. They never reached the Old Town. Another heroic defence made the tower famous in the battles against the Swedes in 1648. But this clash meant the loss of the decoration on the back of the gateway. The ornaments were so badly damaged by the Swedish fire that what remained had to be removed, so it did no further harm.

The Old Town Square with the Town Hall of the Old Town and the Týn church
(Prague 1 – Staré Město)

The Old Town was permitted to have a Town Hall on the basis of a privilege granted by King John of Luxemburg in 1338 and it had a complicated history of merging and rebuilding houses that were gradually bought or donated by the burghers. In the first place there was the house of Volflin of Kamen, acquired by the town in 1338. Over its original Gothic portal there is a renaissance window with the coats of arms of the Roman Empire, the Bohemian kingdom and the Old Town along the sides. The next council house, with a fine renaissance window on the first floor, was bought and added in 1360. Then came the house of the furrier Mikeš, with its neo-renaissance facade. And the town acquired the next-door house to that – At the Sign of the Cock, with a classicist facade, only after 1830. An arcade from the second half of the 14th century was uncovered on the ground floor of these houses.Since 1896 yet another house has been part of the Town Hall – the house At the Sign of the Minute, which juts out into the square. That means that altogether the Town Hall is composed of five houses.

The Tower of the Town Hall

started to be built soon after the Town Hall was founded in 1338. It boasts of an oriel chapel that was consecrated in 1381. In the paving below it (in the direction of Paris boulevard) crosses mark the place where 27 Czech lords were executed in 1621. The famous horologe is to be found on the southern side of the tower.

< The Town Hall Horologe

was made in 1410 by the clockmaker Mikuláš of Kadaň and the astronomer Jan Šindel. In 1490 this "miraculous machine" was repaired by Master Hanuš of Růže. The figures of the apostles, which appear every hour in the clock's window, were added in the 17th century. In the 19th century the horologe was thoroughly repaired and a new calendar panel by the Czech painter Josef Mánes was put in. But the horologe features not only the figures of the apostles, the skeleton, the miser and the profligate, but also the science of astronomy. The astronomical clock shows the years, months, days and hours, the rising and setting of the sun, east and west, the moon and the signs of the Zodiac. A peculiarity is the fact that the Earth is painted in the middle of the clock-face and the sun revolves around it. So the Prague horologe shows the geocentric conception of the universe.

39

The Old Town of Prague

is the oldest of Prague's towns, originating under King Wenceslas I.
in 1232–1234. It still preserves its medieval groundplan, with little winding
streets and picturesque groups of houses of varying ages and styles. Every
house, every stone in the Old Town Square has its history. Even though some of
the houses wear a more modern coat, the core of them all is either Romanesque
or Gothic.

The church of Our Lady Before Týn

(Prague 1 – Staré Město, Staroměstské Square) forms a worthy counterpart to the Town Hall. It was founded at the end of John of Luxemburg's reign and Parléř's works constructed it from 1380. The towers, 80 metres high, end in 4 turrets and spires each with 4 smaller turrets, and between the towers is a late Gothic gable (from 1463). There used to be a statue of the Hussite King George of Poděbrady and a Hussite chalice on this gable. This meant that the Týn church believed in the Reformation. John Huss's predecessors preached in the church: Konrád Waldhauser and Jan Milíč of Kroměříž and even the representative of the radical wing of the German Reformation, Tomáš Münzer. After the Battle of the White Mountain the statue was torn down in 1623 and replaced by one of the Virgin Mary. Her halo was made of the former Hussite chalice.

A little Romanesque church from 1135 used to stand where the Týn church stands today. It belonged to the court for foreign merchants who brought all kinds of goods to Bohemia. Later it was rebuilt in early Gothic style, but in the middle of the 14th century this gave place to the building of a new church, which was only finished at the beginning of the 16th century.

The northern portal of the church is a masterly example of the achievements of Parléř's building works and one of the most valuable high Gothic memorials. The relief over the door represents Christ's crucifixion – the tiny figures are the souls escaping from the dying thieves: devils are fighting over one of them, while angels carry the other to heaven. The entrance to the church is through a passageway in the house of the Týn school. In the interior of the church the main feature is the high altar with its two pictures by Karel Škréta from 1649, The Assumption of the Virgin Mary and The Holy Trinity. The marble tombstone of the Danish astronomer Tychon Brahe is set into the wall behind the Gothic pulpit from the mid 15th century. He was a famous astronomer who served at the court of Emperor Rudolph II., and he was buried here in 1601.

The House At the Sign of the Stone Bell
(Prague 1 – Staré Město, Staroměstské Square)
is called after the stone bell at its corner.
It is one of the most valuable medieval burgher's houses in Prague.
It was built before the end of the 13th century and changed hands
many times. Perhaps even King Charles IV. lived there for a time
when he came to Prague in 1333. The originally Gothic house was
altered and rebuilt by later owners, but has now been returned to its
original form. There are two chapels in the house (on the ground
and first floors) with Gothic murals and fragments of the statues
that used to be on the facade.
(The photograph shows the chapel on the ground floor.)

< The Carolinum – Gothic oriel
(Prague 1 – Staré Město, Ovocný trh [The Fruit Market])
The Carolinum is the oldest preserved university building.
Charles IV. issued the foundation charter of Prague university
in 1348. But then the university had no building of its own – no
lecture halls or studies. Only in 1383 Wenceslas IV. presented
the university with the house of the royal mintmaster and
financier Jan Rotlev, which had two floors in front, three at the
sides and a tall pantiled roof. It contained the oriel chapel of
SS. Cosmas and Damian, richly decorated, which can still be
seen today. There was a large hall on the first floor, which has
also been preserved, though it now has the form given it by
F. M. Kaňka during rebuilding in 1718.
The building was completed round the "court of honour" with a
fountain and granite statues of heraldic lions in 1960 – 69 by
architect Jaroslav Fragner.

The Cross Passage with ribbed vaulting from the 14th and
15th centuries is used for exhibitions.

The Maisel Synagogue (Prague 1 – Staré Město, Maiselova ul.)
was built in 1592 as the private synagogue of the head of the Jewish Town, Mordechai Maisel – court Jew and financier to Emperor Rudolph II. In its day the building amazed people by its size and grandeur.The plans were made by Juda Goldsmied de Herz. Mordechai Maisel and his wife donated many gifts to the synagogue, for instance synagogue curtains, torah crowns and other things.Mordechai Maisel was a truly enlightened man, for he supported the Prague Talmudic school and was known for his generosity in founding various public buildings in the Jewish Town. The synagogue was severely damaged by fire in 1689 and when it was renewed it was considerably smaller. In 1892–1905 it was rebuilt in neo-Gothic style. Nowadays the synagogue is used for exhibitions and as a depository of the Jewish Museum, the latter containing metal objects, mainly silver. The exhibition shows a cross–section of the history of the Jews in Bohemia and Moravia since the 10th century (i.e. since the foundation of the Jewish community here) until the period of emancipation (i.e. till the end of the 18th century).

A silver crown from the collections
of the Jewish Museum.

The Old – New Synagogue (Prague 1 – Staré Město, Červená ulice [Red Street])
The synagogues were the vital centres of the Jewish religious community, the place where decisions were taken on communal affairs and the centre of education and teaching. The Old-New Synagogue is the oldest synagogue to have been preserved in Central Europe. Its toothed brick gable makes a characteristic silhouette. The exterior is a simple oblong building with a tall saddle roof and lean-to additions on three sides. It dates from the last third of the 13th century and was built in early Gothic style. The interior, with two aisles, is arched over with six fields of ribbed vaulting on two mighty pillars. The seats are still placed as they always were, around the walls and facing the centre, where there is a podium with a desk for reading aloud from the torahs. The Old-New Synagogue has always enjoyed great respect and has been wreathed in story and legend. The most important scholars of the Prague Jewish community have been rabbis there: Rabbi Löw, Ezechiel Landau and others.

< **A decorative late Gothic lattice** marks off the most important place in the synagogue, the raised podium for reading aloud from the torah scrolls. It is proof of the high standard of artistry of the medieval craftsmen.

The St. Agnes Convent

(Prague 1 – Staré Město, Anežská Street)
was probably founded in 1231 by King Wenceslas I.
and his sister Agnes (the youngest daughter of King Přemysl
Ottakar I.), who brought the Order of Poor Clares to the convent.
Agnes, who was declared a saint in 1989, was the convent's
first Mother Superior. The convent buildings, surrounding
a cloistered garden, were built from 1233 until the 2nd half
of the 14th century. During the Hussite wars, in 1419 – 1420,
the convent was ransacked and for a time it became
a "military headquarters". In 1436 the nuns returned
to the convent, but in 1782 it was abolished by Joseph II.
and for a long time became a poorhouse.
It was reconstructed in the nineteen-eighties
and the National Gallery.

The Church of St. Francis and the Church of St. Saviour
(Prague 1 – The Old Town, the St. Agnes Convent)
Both churches have just a central nave with interesting tracery and keystones in the vaults.
The church of St. Francis used to be the convent church of the Poor Clares, and only the choir of it survived. It is one of the first early Gothic buildings on the territory of this country, the nave having been consecrated in 1234. The grave of King Wenceslas I. was discovered in the church. Around 1240 Agnes founded a monastery for monks of the Minorite order, in addition to the convent for the nuns. This led to the need for a new church, as the church of St. Francis went to the Minorites, who built a new choir onto it with a pentagonal end around 1250.

The Poor Clares built a new church, that of St. Saviour, which included the chapel of St. Mary Magdalene. This church was to become the mausoleum of the House of Přemyslides. The founding of the mausoleum corresponds to the consecration of the church to Christ the Saviour. This links onto a tradition from the days of Charlemagne (768 – 814), when the western apses of churches, reserved for the rulers of the land, were dedicated to the Saviour. Among the several members of the Přemyslide family buried in the church was also the founder of the convent, Agnes of the Přemyslides, though her grave has never yet been found. The choir of the church has a markedly higher vaulting than the nave of the older church, to which it is linked by a wide, semi–circular arch.

The charming sculptural decoration of the keystones of the arches in the church of St. Saviour consists of the heads of queens.
On one of the capitals there is a portrait of Agnes. Her face tells us that she was a beautiful woman, intelligent and energetic. And this is proved to the full by the work she left behind her.

The Powder Tower (Prague 1 – Staré Město, Celetná Street) originally called the New Tower, was built after 1475 by the builder Matěj Rejsek at the expense of the city. It was built on the site of a former tower, known as "Tattered", which was one of the gates of the Old Town fortifications. The builder Rejsek took as the model and inspiration for his 65 metre high tower Parléř's Old Town Bridge Tower. He too decorated his New Tower, but in a more light-hearted manner. The golden age of this tower was at the end of the 14th century, when the Royal Court (home of the Bohemian kings in Hussite times) grew up next to it (where the Municipal House now stands). When Vladislav II. of the Jagellons – who had himself laid the foundation stone for the New Tower – moved to the Castle, the gateway lost its state importance and its construction came to a halt. It remained unfinished, temporarily roofed over. In 1757, when Prague was besieged by the Prussian army, the tower came down in the world -it was used as a store for gunpowder, and since then it has been named the Powder Tower. In 1875 – 1886 architect Josef Mocker reconstructed the tower. The remains of the original decoration can be seen in the 1st floor interior.

The church of Our Lady of the Snows

(Prague 2 – Nové Město, Jungmannovo Square)
is the tallest church in Prague – the arches being 35 metres high.
It was founded in 1347 by Charles IV. and belonged to the Order of
Carmelites. It was intended to be over 100 metres long and surpass all
other churches in extent and height. In 1397 the tall choir was
completed. In 1419 Wenceslas IV. granted the church to the Utraquists
and it became the main seat and centre of the Hussites. In 1419 – 1422
the priest Jan Želivský preached there. It was he who led a procession
from there to the Town Hall of the New Town in 1419, and there the first
Prague defenestration took place, which led to the beginning of the
Hussite wars. The war put an end to all idea of building a magnificent
church, with its nave where the courtyard now is. The church and the
monastery continued to fall into disrepair until 1604, when the
Franciscans took it over and repaired it. The monastery stands on the
southern side of the church and it has a garden that still forms an oasis
of calm in the midst of the bustle of the city.

In the church interior there is an interesting baroque altar from 1625,
which experts say is the highest altar in the country (as high as
a three-storey house). There is a remarkable Gothic portal
surmounted by a tympanum with a relief from after 1347.

The Bethlehem Chapel (Prague 1 – Staré Město, Betlémské Square)

was built in 1391 to commemorate the Holy Innocents murdered in Bethlehem, where Jesus Christ was born. The chapel was founded by one of the courtiers of King Wenceslas IV., Sir Hanuš of Milheim, and the plot of land on which the chapel stands was donated by an Old Town merchant named Kříž. The chapel was to serve for the preaching of God's word in the Czech language.

From 1402 John Huss looked after the chapel and he also preached there, as did Master Jakoubek of Stříbro – one of the ideological leaders of the Hussite reform movement. The chapel could hold a congregation of some 3,000, and one of them was frequently Queen Sofie (the wife of King Wenceslas IV.)

In 1410 the chapel was to have been closed, because Huss was anathematized for spreading the teachings of Wycliffe. Huss set out for the church council in Constance to defend his teaching, but in 1415 he was burnt at the stake. From 1609 – 1620 the chapel was used by the Union of Brothers. Then after the Thirty Years' War it was transferred to the Jesuits, and in 1786 it was made into an ordinary house. In 1950 – 1954 it was reconstructed by architect Jaroslav Fragner. The remains of inscriptions with Huss's and Jakoubek's tractates can still be seen on the walls.

The Monastery na Slovanech (Emmaus) with the church of the Virgin Mary, St. Jerome and the Slav patron saints (Prague 2 – Nové Město, Vyšehradská)

was founded by Charles IV. in 1347 for the Slav Benedictines from Dalmatia. It was to be a centre of Slavonic learning and literature.

The church is Gothic with a nave and two aisles and ribbed vaulting on eight pillars. Along the whole length of the south side of the church there is a monastery with cloisters under a cross vault. Here part of the famous cycle of murals has been preserved that originally covered all the outer walls of all four wings of the cloisters. These frescos – scenes from the Old and New Testaments – were painted around 1360, and the torso that remains is one of the most important sets of Gothic murals. The monastery was completed in 1372 and it was a centre of education and art up till the Hussite wars. In the 17th century, when it belonged to the Spanish Benedictines, it was refurbished in baroque style. Then after 1880 it was rebuilt as neo-Gothic. In 1945 a bomb fell on the whole building – the church arch was shattered and both towers burnt out. The vaulting and the pillars have been renewed and the towers replaced by new ones, reminiscent of the sails of a ship (designed by architect F. M. Černý).

Prague

RENAISSANCE

The very beginning of the new style, known as Renaissance – 1493 – is written on the facade of the Vladislav hall in Prague Castle. But it seems that this first swallow found its way to our country by mistake. Gothic still ruled in the Czech Lands for several more years. Here we characterize the Renaissance period in our country as the years from 1530 to 1620. After Ferdinand I. of the house of Habsburgs was elected Czech king in1526 there was extensive building activity in Bohemia. Architects and builders came from Italy, bringing the new style with them, and it won immediate support from the royal court and the aristocracy. The years 1537 – 1576 are known in Bohemia as the height of the Renaissance style. The following years – 1576 – 1614 – when the throne was held by Emperor Rudolph II., who again made Prague the centre of Europe, are called the period of late Renaissance or Mannerism.

For Renaissance buildings the measure of everything is man. It is for man that buildings are built, and from this approach it is evident that secular buildings are preferred to ecclesiastical ones. The architecture is tranquil and the horizontal prevails. A typical feature is an attic balustrade. The houses are faced and often graffiti are made by scratching the plaster. The interiors are marked by elaborately coffered ceilings, and a new element is ornamental or geometrical stucco-work, based on ancient Greek models.

The most typical Renaissance memorials in Prague are: the Royal Summer Palace with the Singing Fountain, the Ball–game hall in the Royal Garden of Prague Castle, The Schwarzenberg palace in Hradčany Square, Golden Lane, the Smiřický palace in the Little Quarter Square, the house At the Sign of the Dukes in the Old Town, the house At the Sign of the Two Golden Bears in the Old Town, the house At the Sign of the Minute in the Old Town Square, the Granovský House in Ungelt, the Pinkas synagogue, the Old Jewish cemetery, the Town Hall of the New Town.

The Royal Garden and the Ball-game Hall

(Prague 1 – Hradčany, U Prašného mostu Street)
The Royal Garden was laid out on the site of former vineyards during the reign of Ferdinand I. in 1541, and many rare plants and shrubs were planted there. For the first time precious tulips were grown there. In the baroque period great changes were made and the garden was decorated with statues (for instance the statue of Night by Matyáš Bernard Braun.) Today the garden is laid out as a natural park.

The ball-game hall, where the nobility played games, was built in 1567 – 1569 by architect Bonifác Wohlmut. The graffitos on the facade represent various mythological and allegorical figures.

The Royal Summer Palace
(Prague 1 – Hradčany, Mariánské hradby)
has been called the most beautiful renaissance building north of
the Alps. Ferdinand I. had it built for his wife, whom he is said to have loved
dearly. The design was by Paolo della Stella and the palace was built from
1538 till 1564. It was planned as a place of leisure with a dance hall on
the first floor. It was surrounded with an arcade decorated with a wealth of
figural and ornamental reliefs on subjects from mythology and history,
hunting and other scenes. The roof is in the shape of an up-turned ship's
hull. Standing in the middle of the garden in front of the summer palace is
the Singing Fountain by Francesca Terzia, cast by Tomáš Jaroš in
1564 – 1568. The falling drops of water compose a smiling, pleasurable
melody.

The Hall of the Land Rolls in the Old Palace of Prague Castle

is one of the additions to the parliamentary wing of the Royal Palace, designed and built in 1559 – 1563 by Bonifác Wohlmut. The Land Rolls are books recording all transfers of landed property and estates and the decisions of the Provincial Court, and they have the character of law. The walls of the hall show the coats of arms of the officials of the Land Rolls over the years 1561 – 1774.

The Provincial Diet

served the supreme body of Czech medieval judiciary – the Provincial Court. The scribe sat in the renaissance tribune (from 1564) so that he could go straight into the Land Rolls chamber. The building of the Diet began in 1559 and four years later Bonifác Wohlmut put the late Gothic ceiling over it.

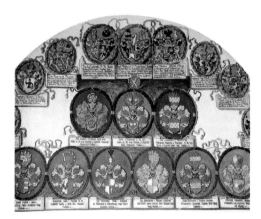

The Schwarzenberg Palace

(Prague 1 – Hradčany, Hradčanské Square 2)
is one of the most beautiful of Prague's palaces, not only because of its rich graffito decoration, but also its exceptional position on the cliff over the castle ramp. The palace was built in 1545 – 1563 from plans by Agostino Galli on the site of four houses that had been burnt down. The extensive building has three wings with a court of honour and gateway. It is covered all over with black and white rustic graffitos, the gables having graffitos of leaves and figures. The interior of the palace has renaissance painted ceilings. The collections of the Military History Museum are housed in the palace.

Golden Lane

is famous for its tiny little houses, in which the castle gunners used to live. The miniature houses were built onto the defence wall from the 16th century. Originally the street was only one metre wide, as there were houses on both sides of it. There was also a women's prison there at one time. The story that during the reign of Rudolph II. the houses were inhabited by alchemists who manufactured gold for the emperor, or the elixir of eternal youth or the philosophers' stone, is only a legend. The poor castle gunners had little chance of discovering anything. As the importance of their profession decreased their curious little houses were lived in by various craftsmen, clerks, bell-ringers and bandmasters, later the Prague poor and people from the underworld. In the 19th century a few people began to appreciate the romantic spell of the place and in the 20th century some famous people lived there – for instance in 1917 Franz Kafka had a study in No.22.

The Velikovský Palace and the Šternberk Palace >
(Prague 1 – Malá Strana, Malostranské Square)
The Velikovský palace was originally a Gothic house with an arcade
and an oriel, decorated with graffitos. But in 1585 it was rebuilt
in renaissance style, and this is the date of the corner oriel. In 1761
the house was bought by František Filip of Šternberk, who owned
the next-door palace. In 1899 the house was repaired and the facade
given new graffito decoration by Celda Klouček. The Šternberk palace
is considered the most beautiful dwelling house in the Little Quarter
Square. It originated by joining 2 renaissance houses (after 1684) and
later adaptation into the present palace, according to plans
by G. B. Alliprandi. In 1562 the head of a Turkish deputation stayed
there, Ibrahim, who came to Prague with 23 servants, 26 horses and
6 camels. There is a picture of the Virgin Mary on the house which,
by an old magisterial decree, is to be kept there for ever.

The Smiřický Palace (The House at the Montagues')
(Prague 1 – Malá Strana, Malostranské Square 18)
is a large building surrounding an inner courtyard, with towers and two
corner oriels. It was built before 1582 and repaired in 1603 – 1613.
It belonged to the richest family in the Bohemia of that time –
the Smiřický family. In 1618 it was the focus of the rising of
the Estates. The Czech lords, led by Albrecht Jan Smiřický, decided to
throw the governor out of the window of the Royal Palace. After
the defeat of the Estates' rising the entire property of the Smiřickýs was
confiscated, and Albrecht of Valdštejn became its new owner.
A later owner of the house was the lord of Montague, who had
an additional storey built onto the house and the whole adapted
in baroque style by the builder J. Jägr.

< The Renaissance window
of the second house of the Town Hall of the Old Town.
This elaborate window, probably built by the Benedikt Ried works
around 1525, is the window of the Wedding Hall. The inscription over
it announces to all and sundry that Prague is the capital city of the
kingdom.

The House At the Sign of the Two Golden Bears
(Prague 1 – Staré Město, Kožná Street 1)
was built on the site of two Gothic houses in 1559 – 1567, partly
by B. Wohlmut. There is a fine renaissance arcade in the courtyard.
The portal, dating from 1570 – 1580, is both decorative and valuable.
The upper part shows two bears approaching from either side a man
holding a branch. The bears used to be gilded.
Alterations in 1683 and especially in 1750 added a storey to the house.
A memorial plaque commemorates the fact that the writer and journalist
Egon Ervin Kisch (1885 – 1948) was born there.

The House at the Sign of the Minute
(Prague 1 – Staré Město, Staroměstské Square) used to have various different names, for instance At the Sign of the White Lion, after a corner sign from the end of the 18th century. The statue of a lion holding a mirror in its front paws recalls a time when there was a pharmacy there. The House at the Sign of the Minute has a Gothic core, but was rebuilt in renaissance style at the end of the 16th century. The figural and ornamental graffitos on the facade illustrate for instance Bacchus's procession or Adam and Eve beneath the forbidden tree.

The House at the Sign of the "U Vejvodů"
(Prague 1 – Staré Město, Jilská Street 4) is one of the oldest Prague houses, as is proved by the cellars that have been preserved and the ground floor of the house. The splendid Renaissance rebuilding after 1618 determined the basic appearance of the house as it is today. The beautiful Renaissance facade with rounded corners is divided by an oriel on cantilevers, and the hall of columns on the ground floor is remarkable for its beauty too. The sign over the portal tells of further rebuilding in the mid 17th century. This sign belonged to Mikuláš František Turek – Mayor of the Old Town – who, like a later owner of the house, also Mayor of the Old Town, Jan Václav Vejvoda excelled in bravery during the defence of the Old Town against the enemy armies of the Swedes and Prussians. This house too contained one of the oldest Prague breweries and a famous inn. Beer has not been brewed there for many years now, but the inn is still famous.

The Granovský's House (Prague 1 – Staré Město, Týnská Street 639)
This house is the entrance to the Týn courtyard – Ungelt – a fenced-off area that was a centre for foreign merchants and a customs house since the 12th century. The original house, where the merchants paid duty on imported goods, was given by Ferdinand I. to the customs officer Jakub Granovský in 1558, and he had it rebuilt to the form it has today with graffitos and murals. The loggia in the courtyard wing is decorated with religious and mythological scenes.

The Jewish Cemetery
(Prague 1 – Staré Město, U starého hřbitova)

is a memorable place of artistically and historically precious gravestones. It was founded at the beginning of the 15th century almost in the centre of the Jewish Town. However it was not the oldest burial ground of the Prague Jewish community. But soon its limited space became too small, and as religious custom forbids disturbing old graves, more and more layers of earth had to be brought to the graveyard so that the dead could be buried in them. So in some places there were as many as twelve burial layers one above the other.

The old gravestones were always lifted to the surface, leading to the piles of stones so characteristic of this unique place. There are now almost 12,000 gravestones in the cemetery, dating from 1439 to 1787, when it was forbidden to bury people in this thickly-populated part of the town. Since the end of the 16th century the tombs were decorated with various symbols and signs, usually showing the origin, name or profession of the deceased. The reliefs of animals mostly express the dead person's name.

The tomb over the grave of Jehuda ben Becalel, known as Rabbi Löw
(1512–1609)
Big four-walled tombs were built over the graves of important persons from the beginning of the 17th century so that there should be more space for texts describing the good deeds of the deceased. Rabbi Low was the head of the Talmudic school in Prague for 36 years and later became chief Rabbi. Here too he published most of his fifteen philosophical and religious books. There are many legends connected with his name, the best known being the story of his creation of an artificial being – Golem.

The Statue of Rabbi Löw
by L. Šaloun from 1910 stands at the corner of the New Town Hall in Marian Square in Prague 1 – The Old Town.
It portrays the Rabbi at the moment when a young girl is giving him a rose in which, legend tells, death was hidden.

The Pinkas Synagogue

(Prague 1 – Staré Město, Široká Street)
was built in 1519 – 1535 as the private place
of prayer for the Hořovský family. Late Gothic
reticulated vaulting arches over the nave.
Between 1607 – 1625 the building was enlarged,
acquiring a hall, an aisle and a women's gallery.
Now the synagogue is a memorial to the 77,297
victims of the Nazi genocide of the Jews in the
Czech Lands. The lists of names inscribed on the
walls of the synagogue are a warning for future
generations.
In the gallery of the synagogue there is an
exibition of children's drawings from the
concentration camp in Terezín from the years
1942 – 1944.

The Town Hall of the New Town (Prague 2 – Nové Město, Karlovo Square)

When Charles IV. founded the New Town of Prague (in 1348) and made Charles Square – then the Cattle Market – the main marketplace of that town, he was well aware that the town would need its Town Hall. And building on it started even during his lifetime – so it still remembers the earliest days of Charles Square. The eastern wing was completed in 1374. In 1411 – 1416 the southern wing, into the square, was built on, and in 1452 the tower, which was also given a horologe. At the beginning of the 16th century the Town Hall was given a renaissance appearance. On the ground floor of the southern wing there is a Gothic hall with two aisles and ribbed vaulting (in the photograph), and in the tower a baroque Lady chapel, which was added in 1622. In the seventeen–eighties the several Prague towns were united and their administration moved to the Town Hall of the Old Town. The Town Hall of the New Town lost its administrative function and became the seat of the penal court.

Prague

BAROQUE

Prague came to know the baroque style from roughly 1611. This novelty quickly put down roots here and dominated for practically the whole of the 17th century and a good part of the 18th. Right from the beginning it developed in two directions: the classicist, linking onto Renaissance and characterized by a sobriety approaching sternness, and the dynamic style, inspired by movement, ferment and exultation.

Whereas the first of these is mainly to be seen in secular architecture, the second is found in ecclesiastical architecture.

The basic sign of baroque architecture is movement in all its forms, spaces mount on and permeate one another, cupolas and windows are used to create a refined play of light. The interiors are decorated with extensive frescos that give an illusion of widening space.

In the period from approximately the end of the 17th century till the middle of the 18th this initially imported style began to take on a Czech colouration, and in the works of its most important representatives – father and son Christopher and Kilián Ignatius Dientzenhofer – achieved a trend that is known as Czech or Prague baroque.

Its characteristic feature is the so–called Czech vault, that arches over the area of any groundplan, thus forming a vast surface for magnificent ceiling paintings, and also generous use of stuccowork, formerly used in interiors, but now adorning the facades of new buildings or completing old ones. The baroque gems of Prague include: Matthias's Gateway in the 1st courtyard of Prague Castle, the church of St. Nicholas in the Little Quarter Square, the Loretta, the church of Our Lady Victorious in Karmelitská Street in the Little Quarter, the church of St. Francis with the monastery of the Knights of the Cross in the Square of the Knights of the Cross, the church of St. Nicholas in the Old Town Square, the church of St. James in Malá Štupartská Street, the church of St. Ignatius in Charles Square, the Clementinum, the Strahov monastery, the Valdštejn palace and garden, the Tuscany palace, the Černín palace, the Archbishop's palace in Hradčany Square, the statues on the Charles Bridge, the Morzini palace in Neruda Street, the Clam–Gallas palace in Huss Street.

The Matthias Gateway to Prague Castle
is the entrance to the grounds of Prague Castle. It was built during the reign of Emperor Matthias in 1614 by the architect G. M. Filippi, and is the oldest baroque building in Prague.

The statues of the Giants over the Gateway to Prague Castle
The figures of the fighting giants were made by the sculptor Ignác Platzer the elder in 1768.

The Archbishop's Palace

(Prague 1 – Hradčany, Hradčanské Square)
The original seat of the Prague bishops, from the 10th to the end of the 12th century, was a house within the Castle (where the old Provost's House now stands). In the following centuries the bishops – and since 1344 archbishops – had their seat in the Bishop's Court (near the Judith and later Charles Bridge). The Bishop's Court was destroyed in 1419, but King Ferdinand I. only gave the Prague archbishop a house in Hradčany Square in 1562. Originally it was a renaissance house, but in the second half of the 17th century it was adapted in baroque style by architect J. B. Mathey, at the wish of archbishop Jan Bedřich of Valdštejn. The present rococo appearance of the palace was given it by architect Jan Josef Wirch. He respected his predecessor's baroque architecture, but added rococo decorations. The rococo style is more in evidence in the interior (the staircase, the interiors of the salons). The palace's treasures include a set of eight French tapestries from 1754 – 1765, with exotic motifs on the theme New India.

The Tuscany Palace (Prague 1 – Hradčany, Hradčanské Square)
forms a fitting counterpart to the Castle at the opposite end of Hradčany Square. It was built in monumental Roman baroque style in 1689 – 1691 by J. B. Mathey and G. Canevalle on the site of several burghers' and aristocrats' houses. The palace belonged to Michal Osvald, Count Thun–Hohenštejn, who had a library and valuable collections there. In 1718 the Thun–Hohenštejns sold the palace to the Grand Duchess Maria Anna of Tuscany. It is an imposing building with four wings and a newly symmetrically planned facade with two little towers.

The seven statues on the roof, between the towers, represent free art and are the work of Jan Brokof. It is this sculptural decoration of the roof that gives the Tuscany Palace its resemblance to the 17th century Roman palaces. There is also a statue of the archangel Michael – the builders' patron – on the corner of the palace. This is by Ottavio Mosto and dates from 1693.

The Černín Palace (Prague 1 – Hradčany, Loretánské Square)
This building, which is 150 metres long, is said to have as many windows as there are days in the year.
The imperial envoy to Venice, Humprecht Jan Černín of Chudenice and his son Heřman Černín, had it built in
1668 – 1697. The architect Francesco Caratti made the plans in Palladian Renaissance style. After his death
the building work was overseen by Giovanni Maderna, and after him again by Domenico Rossi. Typical features
of the palace are its rustication, the 32 huge half-columns and extensive balcony. Those who took a share in
the interior decoration include the sculptor Matyáš Bernard Braun and V. V. Reiner. The palace has a beautiful
garden that screens two salla terrenas, an orangery and pools.

The Loretto (Prague 1 – Hradčany, Loretánské Square)

The Loretto or Santa Casa is the name given to the little house in the centre of the compound. Legend tells that the cottage in which the Virgin Mary dwelt in Nazareth with the little Jesus was brought by angels to Italy in 1291 and thus was saved from the infidels who occupied the Holy Land. The name of the place they brought it to was Loretto near Ancona. The little house was greatly venerated and copies of it were built all over Europe in the baroque period. The Loretto cottage in Prague was built in 1626 – 1627 by Giovanni Battista Orsi at the expense of Katherine of Lobkovicz. Fifty years later this much frequented place was surrounded by cloisters and then given an additional storey. The cloisters have painted ceilings and there are six chapels in the corners and the middles of the shorter sides. The one that is most visited is that with a statue of the crucified bearded woman saint, St. Starosta. The church of the Nativity with the entrance facade and towers was built by Kilian Ignác Dientzenhofer in 1734 – 1735. A carillon rings out from the tower every hour. This was ordered at the end of the 17th century by a burgher of the Little Quarter from the bell-founder of Amsterdam, Claudius Fromm. The mechanism was constructed by the Prague clockmaker Petr Neumann.

The Loretto Treasure

The famous treasury with liturgical objects from the 16th – 18th centuries is on the first floor over the cloisters. The best known treasure is the diamond monstrance, made in 1696 – 1699 of heavily gilded silver and set with 6,222 diamonds. It was made by the goldsmiths Matthias Stegner and Johann Khünichbauer and weighs 12 kilograms. Another monstrance is set with 260 diamonds and great quantities of pearls, so it is called the pearl monstrance. Other monstrances again, with names such as the hawthorn wreath or the ringlet monstrance, are no less beautiful. The oldest item in the treasury is a gilded silver Gothic chalice from 1510, decorated with pictures of the Bohemian patron saints.

There are also some valuable pictures in the treasury, one of the most remarkable being a picture of the Madonna with a wreath of vines, painted on wood. There are other valuable things in the Loretto treasury too, silver reliquaries with relics of saints, precious goblets, robes for the mass. Golden crowns, intended to crown statues of the Virgin Mary and the little Jesus, are especially splendid. They are most of them gifts from the noblewomen of the leading Czech families.

The Strahov Monastery

The entrance to the monastery is a baroque gateway with a statue of St. Norbert, founder of the Order of Premonstratensians. Beyond this is the little church of St. Roch, built at the beginning of the 17th century in a strange combination of Gothic and Renaissance. Nowadays it is an exhibition hall known as the Musaion.

The monastery was founded in 1140 beside an important road leading to the Castle. The founder, at the instigation of the Olomouc bishop Jindřich Zdík, was Prince Vladislav II himself, and thanks to the royal favour the monastery flourished and soon became a centre of learning, famous for its library. The Prince and his wife liked to visit the monastery, and they are both buried there. The original Romanesque compound (1142 – 1182) was damaged several times, so it was often rebuilt. Its appearance today is baroque, but numerous remains of the Romanesque building have been preserved, including two complete rooms.

< The Abbey Church of the Assumption of the Virgin Mary

is fundamentally a Romanesque basilica from the 12th century, but rebuilt in Renaissance and baroque styles. The interior decoration is mainly baroque, dating from around 1750. The relics of St. Norbert are laid on the main altar of the chapel of St. Ursula.

On the first floor of the monastery is the **Theological Hall**, originally the monastery library, built in 1671 – 1679 by G. D. Orsi. Siard Nosecký painted pictures in the arche connected with the theme of librarianship. The valuable baroque shelves contain numerous theological books, manuscripts and first prints.

The Philosophical Hall, built in 1782 – 1784 by architect Ignác Palliardi, has a building to itself. It contains ceiling paintings by A. F. Maulbertsch from 1794 on the subjec of Man's Struggle for the Knowledge of True Wisdom.

Detail of the frescos in the Theological Hall of Strahov Library. When the monastery was rebuilt at the end of the 17th century, the Theological Hall of the library was built by G. D. Orsi in 1671 – 1679 and richly decorated with paintings. The frescos from 1723 – 27 are by Siard Nosecký.

An Antiphonary from the beginning of the 16th century, one of the proofs that tell of the wealth of the collections in the Strahov library.

< Portal with Giants of the Clam-Gallas Palace
(Prague 1 – Staré Mésto, Husova Street 20)
This high baroque palace was built in 1715 – 1730
from plans by architect Jan Fischer of Erlach.
The striking feature of the facade are the two portals,
with two pairs of giants bearing the capitals of
Tuscany columns. Resting on these is a balcony with
vases and figures of children. The sculptor was
Matyáš Bernard Braun, who also decorated the vast
staircase in the interior. There is a fine hall in the
palace that was used for plays or concerts. In 1796
Ludwig van Beethoven conducted there.

A Moor from the Morzini Palace
(Prague 1 – Malá Strana, Nerudova Street 5)
This palace was built on the site of four older houses
and the appearance it presents today was given it by
architect Jan Aichl Santini in 1713 – 1714. Ferdinand
Maxmilian Brokof decorated the facade with statues
of Moors, allegorical busts of Day and Night on
the first floor, a plastic Moorish coat of arms in the
middle of the facade and allegorical statues of four
continents on the attic.

The church of St. Nicholas in the Little Quarter >
(Prague 1 – Malá Strana, Malostranské Square)
This church is a peak example of Prague baroque and it is
the dominant of the Little Quarter. It divides the square into two parts.
It was built in 1704 – 1756 on the site of a demolished Gothic church
of the same name. Those who took a share in building it were: Kryštof
Dientzenhofer (the nave), Kilián Ignác Dientzenhofer (the choir and
the dome), Anselm Lurago (the slender tower).

The ceiling fresco in the nave on the Glorification of St. Nicholas
is by Jan Lukáš Kracker from 1761. The frescos in the dome – celebrating
the Holy Trinity-are by František Xaver Balko from 1751. The four large
statues of the Church Fathers and the gilded statue of St. Nicholas
on the main altar are by Ignác Platzer from 1752 – 1755. The organ dates
from the middle of the 18th century and Mozart played it.

The Valdštejn Palace
(Prague 1 – Malá Strana, Valdštejnské Square 4)

The palace of Albrecht of Valdštejn, generalissimo of the imperial armies, is the biggest of Prague's baroque palaces. In 1623 – 1630 Duke Valdštejn had this spreading palace built with five courtyards and a garden. This was during the Thirty Years' War. Andrea Spezza and Niccolo Sebregondi took part in the building, which was overseen by Giovanni Pieroni. Owing to the size of the palace it was built in several stages, being shut off from the outer world, concentrated around the architectonically planned gardens and courtyards. The palace facade is 60 metres long and occupies the whole of one side of the square. A remarkable large hall – **the Knights' Hall** – occupying two storeys, is decorated with stucco work and frescos depicting Valdštejn as the god Mars in a triumphal chariot.. These are by the Italian artist Baccio Bianco. The palace chapel of St. Wenceslas contains the oldest baroque altar in Prague, dating from 1630.

The Valdštejn Palace Garden (Prague 1 – Malá Strana, Letenská Street)
was laid out in the style of a French baroque park with cut shrubs and contrived views through to little statues or fountains. Work on making the garden started in 1623, according to a project by Andrea Spezza, and it was completed within four years. There is an alley through the centre of the western part of the garden lined with bronze statues by Adrian de Vries, considered the height of European Mannerism. However, those in the garden today are only copies, as the originals were taken off in 1648 by the Swedish army as the booty of war. Passing Venus's fountain one comes to the salla terrena. This is one of the most valuable buildings of the palace compound, created in the spirit of late Italian Renaissance by G. Pieroni. The large columned hall has ceiling stucco work and pictures on the theme of the Trojan war. A typical feature of all baroque gardens – and so too of the Valdštejn garden – was an artificial cave – a grotto.

The church of Our Lady Victorious (Prague 1 – Malá Strana, Karmelitská Street)

said to be the first of Prague's baroque churches. It was built in 1611 – 1613 from plans by G. Maria Filippi for the German Lutherans. In 1624 it came into the possession of the Order of the Bare–footed Carmelites. The church is interesting for having an unusually situated main altar – facing west, and a lofty eastern facade giving onto the street. The new facade, built in 1634 – 1644 with a baroque portal, then became a model for other baroque portals. There is a crypt under the church.

The Prague Child Jesus (Bambino di Praga)

This little wax statue has made the church world-famous. It was brought from Spain at the end of the 16th century and in 1628 Lady Polyxena of Lobkovicz gave it to the Carmelites. The Child Jesus has many changes of costume throughout the year, donated by individuals and organizations from all over the world.

The Statues on the Charles Bridge

form a unique outdoor gallery. Most of them come from the end of the 17th and beginning of the 18th centuries and there are altogether 30 of them. The ardent gestures or, on the contrary, expressions of humble resignation to fate, tell the stories of the rows of saints.

One of the best-known groups of statues on the bridge is that of St. John de Matha, St. Felix of Valois (a member of the Order of Trinitarians) and St. Ivan the Hermit. These three attempted to buy a group of Christians out of Turkish imprisonment. The statue is commonly known as "the Prague Turk", after the Turk who is guarding the Christians. The sculptor was F. M. Brokof and it dates from 1714.

Between the statue of St. John the Baptist (on the 7th pillar on the right, going from the Old Town Bridge Tower) and the next statue there is a marble plaque in the wall inset with a metal cross and five stars. This marks the place where St. John of Nepomuk was hurled into the water. The statue of St. John of Nepomuk dates from 1683 and it was cast from a model by Jan Brokof.

One of the most effective groups is The Dream of St. Luitgarde by Matyáš Bernard Braun from 1710. It tells the story of a blind Cistercian nun who had a vision that Christ was bending down to her from the cross.

< The oldest sculpture on the bridge is the Calvary on the 4th pillar on the right, going from the Old Town Bridge Tower. When the building of the bridge was finished a cross was set up at this place. This was perhaps because the opposite ledge was used as an execution ground. Before losing his head the victim knelt by the cross to pray for the last time. The bronze statue of Christ that hangs on the cross today was cast in Dresden in 1629 and was placed on the bridge in 1657. The gilded Hebrew inscription glorifying God was paid for from the fine levied on a Jew, who is said to have mocked the cross. The statues at the sides, of St. John the Evangelist and the Virgin Mary, are by Emanuel Max from 1861.

**The church of St. Francis and the monastery of the
Knights of the Cross with a Red Star in
the Square of the Knights of the Cross**
(Prague 1 – Staré Město)
The dome of the church of St. Francis stands
up proudly in the little square that is famed for its
beauty. The church was built by architect Canevallo from
plans by J. B. Mathey in 1679 – 1689.
The groundplan of the church is an equilateral
cross – the symbol of the Order, but it faces north
instead of east. There are statues by Ondřej
Quitainer from 1758 in the niches on the facade and on
the cornice. Beneath the church lies the original church of
the Holy Ghost, of which the Gothic ribbed vaulting has
been preserved and part of
a Romanesque column.
The church belongs to the only Czech Order, which
originated as a hospice brotherhood in 1234 and
became an independent Order in 1237. Its main
mission was keeping a hospice and, thanks to its
position, also looking after the stone Judith Bridge.

The frescos in the dome, representing the Last
Judgment are by the Czech painter V. V. Reiner. >

The Clementinum (Prague 1 – Staré Město, Křižovnická Street)

originally a large Jesuit college, it was built on the site of 32 houses, 3 churches, 2 gardens and a place destroyed by fire.
But the place where the compound of buildings stands today was partly built up even in the 12th century. The church of St. Clement stood where the presbytery of the church of St. Saviour now is, and beside it the Dominicans built a monastery, later destroyed by the Hussites. The Jesuits came to Prague in 1556 and they built on the ruins of earlier buildings the most extensive architectural unit in old Prague, except for the Castle. They started teaching there and their college had all the rights of university. Their property grew in size and in the variety of activities there, for instance from 1558 till 1700 there was a theatre in the college. And so great was the crowd that came to the performances that they were moved from the Clementinum courtyard to the Square of the Knights of the Cross.
In 1648 the Jesuits helped defend the city against the Swedes. That is why, in the garden beside the entrance from Křižovnická Street, there is a statue of a student by E. Max, made in 1848 to commemorate the fight of the students two centuries earlier in defence of Prague.

The western wing of the college – in the direction of the Square of the Knights of the Cross – was built in 1653 by Francesco Caratti, and a further wing was finished by 1726, from plans by F. M. Kaňka. Also within the grounds of the Clementinum there is a remarkable church dedicated to St. Clement. This was rebuilt in 1711 – 1715 by F. M. Kaňka. In the dome there are four frescos depicting the life of St. Clement, and on the balcony there is a statue of him with four angels. Beside the exit into Charles Street, and under the same portico, is the entrance to a lovely Italian chapel from 1600.

In the third courtyard there is an observatory with a metal **statue of Atlas** on the top of the tower. Meteorological records have been kept in the observatory in the tower for over 200 years. Nowadays the National Library of the Czech Republic is housed in the Clementinum, which owns many precious books.

The Baroque Library Hall of the Clementinum

The library began to be built in 1722 from plans by F. M. Kaňka. The hall has a rounded arch with three fields, painted in 1727 by J. Hiebel. The frescos in the southern half represent the allegory of Science Apprehended by Reason (a discussion between astronomers, musicians and figures symbolizing the various branches of science), and the northern half is devoted to the Discovery of Truth – theology (The Transfiguration of Christ, spiritual dignitaries).

The Mirror Chapel of the Clementinum

The chapel of the Annunciation of the Virgin Mary, built in 1724, is richly adorned, and gets its name from the mirrors placed along the windowless side. It is now used as a concert hall.

The House At the Sign of the Golden Well

(Prague 1 – Staré Město, Karlova Street)

This is one of the most picturesque Old Town houses. It is worth noticing not only for its peculiar groundplan, but for the wealth of decoration on the facade (looking towards the Charles Bridge), full of stucco figures. Over the windows at the top lies St. Rosalia in a kind of cave, on the 3rd floor are St. Ignatius and St. Francis Xavier, below them St. Wenceslas and St. John of Nepomuk, and below them the Virgin Mary of Boleslav being crowned by angels and the date 1701. Beside the windows on the Ist floor are St. Sebastian and St. Roch (the saint who protects people from the plague).

The House At the Sign of the Golden Grapes

(Prague 1 – Malá Strana, Malostranské Square)

forms the corner of the Little Quarter Square and Carmelite Street, reaching hous No. 516 – the remains of the former Oujezd gateway and tower – part of the fortifications of the Little Quarter, with which it forms a disparate whole. The attractive crookedness of the house gives it a special character; originally it was Gothic, but was rebuilt in renaissance style. Later again, in 1707–1710, it wa given today's baroque appearance by Jan Josef Mayer. Behind its interesting facade with three medallions and a corner sign, the house has an interesting interior with painted renaissance ceilings on two floors.

The church of St. Nicholas in the Old Town Square (Prague 1 – Staré Město, U radnice 1)
Like most baroque churches this one too was originally Gothic, and in 1635 a monastery of the Order
of Benedictines was built beside it. The church was rebuilt in high baroque style in 1732 – 1735 by Kilián Ignác
Dientzenhofer. As the entrance to the church faced a narrow little street of the Jewish Town, there was no need
for any special decoration. However, the side facing the Town Hall is bountifully decorated, giving the impression
that the main entrance is there. The interior is generously adorned with stucco work and a baroque fresco by
Cosmas Damian Assam with scenes from the lives of St. Nicholas and St. Benedict.

The church of St. James

(Prague 1 – Staré Město, Štupartská Street)
is the longest church in Prague after the St. Vitus
cathedral. It has a nave and two aisles, originally
Gothic, as it was founded, together with
a Minorite monastery, in 1232. During the reign of
Charles IV. it was rebuilt at great cost. After
a fire in 1689 it was again rebuilt by Jan
Šimon Pánek.
The stucco decoration on the church's facade is
the work of the baroque sculptor Ottavio Mosto
from 1695. Over the main entrance stands
the figure of St. James in traditional pilgrim's garb
with a staff in his hand, over the right
entrance is St. Francis and over the left
St. Anthony of Padua.

The interior of the church has rich baroque
decoration. The ceiling frescos are by F. Voget
from 1736, and they show scenes from the life of
the Virgin Mary over the nave and
the Celebration of the Holy Trinity in
the presbytery. Over the main altar hangs a
picture of the Torture of St. James by V. V. Reiner.
In the left-hand aisle there is a fine baroque tomb
of the Supreme Bohemian Chancellor, Václav
Vratislav of Mitrovice, designed by the Viennese
architect Jan Bernard Fischer of Erlach,
the statues on the tomb being by Ferdinand
Maxmilian Brokof.

(Prague 2 – Nové Město, Karlovo Square)

...as built on the site of the original Gothic church which Ferdinand II. gave the Jesuits in 1623 together with the plot of land. The Jesuits took an eager part in the building of the New Town. First they started to build the Jesuit College (now the Faculty Hospital) and in 1665 – 1687 they built this massive church, designed by the architect Carlo Lurago. The facade has rich stucco decoration and on top of the church a statue of St. Ignatius, founder of the Order of Jesuits, shines in a golden aureole. In 1697 – 1699 the church was altered by Pavel Ignác Bayer after the model of the Old Town church of St. Saviour by having a distinctive portico added in front of the facade. On the balcony over the portico there is a statue of the Saviour bearing the cross and images of the eight saints of the Jesuit Order. The wide nave of the church is bordered with dimly lit side chapels, intended for private prayer or reflection. The huge main altar of the portal type is from the 2nd half of the 18th century and the picture over it is of the Apotheosis of St. Ignatius by Jan Jiří Heintsch from 1688.

Prague

CLASSICIST, ROMANTIC, ART NOUVEAU AND MODERN

The style of the last third of the 18th century is known as Classicism. Memorials built in this style are sober. Inspiration from ancient Greece is evident in the facades with columns and low triangular gables. Such buildings include for instance: the Estates Theatre, the Strahov library, the house At the Sign of the Hybernians in the Square of the Republic and Bertramka.

For almost the whole of the second half of the 19th century and the beginning of the 20th buildings were put up in historical styles – imitations of all of them. For churches Romanesque and Gothic styles were recommended, for castles, town halls, museums and schools it was Renaissance, and towards the close of the 19th century even baroque was used for residential houses. The architecture for these neo–styles was plentifully decorated with paintings and sculptures.

Prague monuments of this period include: the National Theatre, the National Museum, the Rudolfinum, the Smetana Museum, the church of SS. Peter and Paul in Vyšehrad, the Spanish synagogue.

The style called Art Nouveau made its entry to this country in the mid eighteen–nineties, and it lasted till the nineteen–twenties. The adherents of this new style insisted on untraditional décor and laid stress on detail. The ornamentation of Art Nouveau is full of elegant curves and curls unparalleled in previous styles. A typical element of any Art Nouveau facade is asymmetry. The most beautiful Art Nouveau buildings in Prague are: the Municipal House of the City of Prague, the Evropa Hotel in Wenceslas Square, the main railway station (the Wilson station), the House of the Hlahol Choir on the Masaryk Embankment, the Huss memorial in the Old Town Square, the Svatopluk Čech Bridge, the Industrial Palace in the Exhibition Grounds in Prague 7 – Holešovice.

A unique feature of Czech architecture are buildings in Cubist style. Cubist architecture is pliant, expressively modelled of diffracted, rising and falling surfaces, divided diagonally or by rays, recalling and causing sharp lines of light and shade. Cubist buildings in Prague include: the House At the Sign of the Black Mother of God in Celetná Street, the triple family house on the Rašín Embankment and others.

Architecture of the period between the two World Wars is known mainly as Functionalism. These buildings are remarkable for their geometrical shapes, with flat roofs and broad windows, sometimes entire glass facades. The whole of this period was influenced, both theoretically and practically, by the French architect le Corbusier.

In this book this style is represented by the house of the Society of Artists, called Mánes on the Masaryk Embankment.

Contemporary architecture to be found in Prague attempts to link onto Czech modern architecture, which was of world standard from the end of last century up till the Second World War. In this book excellent new buildings are represented by that of the Nationale Nederlanden on the Rašín Embankment.

The Estates Theatre (Prague 1 – Staré Město, Ovocný trh 6)

was built in 1781 – 1783 according to plans by the architect Antonín Haffenecker at the expense of Count F. A. Nostic, in the then new style – classicism. It was then bought by the Czech Estates. In January 1787 the audience went wild with enthusiasm over the performance of Mozart's The Marriage of Figaro, and in October of the same year the first performance of his opera Don Giovanni was given in this theatre with the composer himself conducting. And in honour of the coronation of Emperor Leopold II. as king of Bohemia the first performance of Mozart's La Clemenza di Tito also took place here in 1791.
It was from the stage of the Estates Theatre too that the song "Where Is My Home" was first sung in 1834 (from Tyl's and Škroupa's comedy "Fidlovačka") that later became the Czech national anthem.

The House At the Sign of the Hibernians
(Prague 1 – Nové Město, Republika Square 3)

The place where this house stands today has a very varied history.

Under Charles IV. there was a Benedictine monastery there with its church of St. Ambrose. The stormy days that followed the death of Wenceslas IV. (son of Charles IV.) led to the monks being thrown out and the monastery destroyed. Then in 1630 Irish Franciscan monks, exiled from Britain by the Protestant Queen Elizabeth I., arrived in Prague and took over the site. The name of the house and the neighbouring street is taken from the Latin name for Ireland (Hibernia).

The Franciscans were given the land by Emperor Ferdinand II., as it had belonged to their predecessors. Aware that they should be useful to the public the Hibernians (as people had begun to call them) started teaching in their monastery. Soon they gained a powerful patron, and thanks to his financial aid were able to build a new monastery and church, which they dedicated to the Immaculate Conception of the Virgin Mary. It was probably built by Carlo Lurago and was completed in 1659. The monks started to cultivate potatoes in the large monastery garden. At first people distrusted this unknown vegetable, but that was soon overcome and in a short time potato-growing spread all over Bohemia.

However in 1786 Joseph II. abolished the monastery and the monks returned to their former home. The place they left then served quite worldly pleasures. In 1792–1802 there was a theatre there. Extensive adaptations were made in 1808 – 1811 by architect Jiří Fischer in the Empire style, and the buildings were used as a finance office and customs house.

The latest changes were made in 1940 – 1942, when the house was made into an exhibition hall.

Bertramka (Prague 5 – Smíchov, Mozartova 2) is a delightful Prague homestead now forever linked with the name of Mozart. According to old etchings it used to lie in the midst of vineyards, and the drive up to it was lined with chestnut trees. It was built at the beginning of the 17th century on the site of an old wooden vintner's house. It is named after one of its many owners, František of Bertram or Pertran. Following several other owners the house was bought in 1784 by the famous opera singer Josefina Dušková. In 1787 and 1791 Mozart was a guest of the Dušeks and, besides other compositions he composed the overture to Don Giovanni here. Today Bertramka is kept as a memorial to Mozart and the Dušeks and concerts are held in the garden – weather permitting.

(Prague 1 – Staré Město, Alšovo nábřeží 12)
is a neorenaissance building, highly decorated with sculptures and graphic works by the leading artists of its day. It was built in 1876 – 1884 from plans by architects Josef Zítek and Josef Schulz as a building for various cultural entertainments. In the southern part there is a fine concert hall with excellent acoustics – the Dvořák Hall – where concerts of the Prague Spring Music Festival have been held every year since 1946.

In the northern part there are art galleries. Two stone sphinxes guard the entrance to the building, and the steps to the southern part are guarded by two seated female figures representing secular and spiritual music. The statues on the attic storey are of famous musicians and artists.

The Smetana Museum (Prague 1 – Staré Město, Novotného lávka 1) originally the administrative building of the Prague waterworks, it was built in 1887 in Czech neorenaissance style by architect Antonín Wiehl. The facade is covered with black and white graffitos, the ornamental part of the decoration having been designed by architect Jan Koula, and the figural part by the 19th century Czech painters František Ženíšek and Mikoláš Aleš on the theme The Defence of the Old Town of Prague from the Swedes in 1648, during the Thirty Years' War. Only in 1935 the town succeeded in having the building made into the Bedřich Smetana Museum. The exhibits tell of the life and work of the Czech musical genius Bedřich Smetana. There is a hall with very good acoustics where concerts are held, mainly of Smetana's music. In front of the museum, on the broad end of the Novotný Footbridge, there is a memorial to Smetana by the sculptor J. Malejovský.

Vyšehrad

(Prague 2 – Nové Město, Vyšehrad)
Originally the site of Slav and medieval castles but which is more linked in people's minds with the lives of the legendary Bohemian princes. The first written report of the existence of Vyšehrad is an entry in Cosmas's Chronicle from 1003. Between the 10th and 12th centuries it was the second Prague seat of the Přemyslides, and it was indeed well chosen for it towered on a high cliff over the river so that access to it was difficult. Vyšehrad is dominated by the pseudo-Gothic towers of the **church of SS. Peter and Paul**, founded by Prince Vratislav II. around 1070. It has been rebuilt many times, most recently in 1885 – 1903 according to plans by J. Mocker in neo-Gothic style.

In the Vyšehrad orchards there are statues by J. V. Myslbek on subjects from Czech mythology (Ctirad and Šárka, **Slavoj and Záboj**, Přemysl and Libuše and others). A memorial place in Vyšehrad is the Pantheon in the cemetery there. This is the last resting place of important personalities of Czech political, social and cultural life.

The National Theatre (Prague 1 – Nové Město, Národní třída 2)
is of special significance for the Czech nation. In the middle of the 18th century Prague had no theatre that played only in Czech. The Czech language could be heard occasionally in some theatres, but mostly plays were in German. In the rousing atmosphere of realization of a national identity collections were made all over the country, with the slogan "The nation to itself", to build a Czech national theatre. In 1868 the foundation stone was ceremonially laid. The building – in late renaissance style from plans by architect Josef Zítek – was completed in 1881, but as craftsmen were finishing off the roof a fire broke out, owing to negligence, that destroyed the stage and the auditorium. A new collection was made and in 1883 the building was again ready for use, this time from plans by architect Josef Schulz.

The exterior sculptural decoration includes a "triga" or three-in-hand on the pylons of the main facade (by Ladislav Šaloun, from a design by Bohumil Schnirch) and statues on the embankment facade by J.V. Myslbek and Antonín Wagner. The interior decoration displays the best that Czech 19th century art created. The artist Mikoláš Aleš, František Ženíšek, Josef Tulka, Vojtěch Hynais, Julius Mařák, Václav Brožík, Adolf Liebscher, and the sculptors Bohumil Schnirch, J. V. Myslbek, Antonín Wagner, Ladislav Šaloun, Josef Mařatka, Jan Štursa, Bohumil Kafka and others compose what is known as the generation of National Theatre artists.

Wenceslas Square (Prague 2 – Nové Město) >

was one of the three centres of the New Town, founded in 1348 by
Charles IV., and also the main link between the Old and New
Towns. It was then called the Horse Market. Where the National
Museum stands today there was the gateway of St. Prokop, or the
Horse Gateway. There were two fountains in the square, but there
were also two gallows and a pillory.
Now Wenceslas Square is the main Prague artery, and there is a
special symbolic place (beneath the statue of St. Wenceslas)
dedicated to the memory of all the victims of the totalitarian regime.
The square is 750 metres long and 60 metres wide. It is named
after the equestrian memorial to Prince
Wenceslas, surrounded by statues of the four Czech patron saints:
St. Ludmila, St. Prokop, St. Agnes and St. Adalbert, all of them by
J. V. Myslbek from 1912 – 1924. Across the top of the square is the
imposing building of the National Museum, designed by architect
J. Schulz and built in 1885 – 1890. On both sides the square is
lined with shops, banks, hotels and other institutions.

The Spanish Synagogue

was built in 1868 in neo–Renaissance style with Moorish elements from plans Vojtěch Ignác Ullmann and Josef Niklas. The rich ornamentation of the interior originated in 1882 – 1893 according to designs by Antonín Baum and Bedřich Münzberger. The facade is designed as tiered architecture with much stucco decoration. The Ark of the Covenant is located over the central window. The synagogue stands on the site of the demolished Old School, which is said to be the oldest Jewish place of prayer in Prague (from the 12th century). The permanent exhibition in the nave and the gallery of the synagogue is entitled The History of the Jews in Bohemia and Moravia from the Emancipation to the Present Day. This links onto the exhibition in the Maisel synagogue.

Paris Boulevard (Prague 1 – Staré Město, Pařížská třída)

the first Prague boulevard lined with residential houses built in historical and Art Nouveau styles. It originated owing to the sanitation of Josefov after 1896 (Prague's Jewish Town) of which only a few synagogues, the Town Hall and the cemetery remained.

The Municipal House of the Capital City of Prague (Prague 1 – Staré Město, Republika Square)
This splendid Art Nouveau building, built from plans by the architects Antonín Balšánek and Osvald Polívka in 1905 – 1911, stands on a memorable site – it is the place where the Royal Court stood, the residence of the Bohemian kings, set up by Wenceslas IV. when Prague Castle had been destroyed by fire. Several further kings lived in the Royal Court until, in 1483, King Vladislav II. of the Jagellons moved back to Prague Castle. The buildings then changed hands and gradually became dilapidated till in 1903 they were demolished and this Art Nouveau building took their place, forming a perfect composition with the next-door historical Powder Tower. Both the exterior and the interior are adorned with works of art by the most important artists of the time.

Over the portal is a large mosaic "Homage Prague" by Karel Špillar. The same artist decorated the Smetana Hall – the concert hall of the Municipal House – with allegoric pictures representing Music, the Dance, Poetry and Drama on the walls of the side balconies, and in the vault there is a figural painting by František Ženíšek. The salons and club-rooms are decorated with the work of the sculptors: J. Mařatka, L. Šaloun, J. V. Myslbek and the artists: A. Mucha, M. Švabinský, J. Panuška, M. Aleš and others.

The House of the Hlahol Choir
(Prague 2 – Nové Město, Masarykovo nábřeží No. 248)
was built in 1904 – 1905 from plans by architect Josef Fanta for the famous
Song Group Hlahol. The sculptured figures on the facade are by Josef
Pekárek and the ornaments by Karel Mottl. There are three memorial plaques
commemorating famous choir-masters (Bedřich Smetana, Karel Bendl and
Karel Knittl). The side facing Vojtěšská Street is also highly decorated.

The Industrial Palace – The Exhibition Ground

(Prague 7 – Holešovice, Výstaviště)
was built in 1891 from plans by architect Bedřich Münzberger for
the Jubilee National Exhibition in 1891. The Art Nouveau adaptations were
carried out in 1897 and 1898, planned by the architects B. Ohmann and
A. Dryák, and later adaptations were made in 1907 by Josef Fanta. In 1991
the whole area was replanned again – including the famous Křižík's
Fountains – for the Czechoslovak Jubilee Exhibition 1991.

Bílek's Villa (Prague 1 – Hradčany, Mickiewiczova Street 1) is the villa that belonged to the sculptor, artist and architect František Bílek, who designed it himself, including the interiors and the furniture in 1911. The theme of the whole house is a field of corn. The pillars at the entrance are stylized ears of corn and there are similar motifs in the interior.

One of František Bílek's main works stands on the steps in front of the villa: a sandstone sculpture **"Comenius Bids Farewell to his Country"** (from 1926). The villa is open to the public and is a memorial to the artist and symbolist František Bílek.

The House At the Sign of the Black Mother of God
(Prague 1 – Staré Město, Celetná Street 34)

This is one of the few Cubist houses in Prague. Cubism is a trend unusual in architecture, aimed at shaping everything into basic geometrical form: squares, circles, spheres, prisms, triangles, cones and cubes. The facades of houses were divided according to diagonals or rays, to give the full effect of the sharp lines between light and shade.

The House At the Sign of the Black Mother of God was built in 1911 – 1912 from plans by Josef Gočár. The name of the house comes from an old house sign from the 17th century. Today it houses the Museum of Czech Modern Art, including a permanent exhibition of Czech Cubism.

A Triple Family House on the Rašín Embankment

(Prague 2 – Nové Město, Rašínovo nábřeží č. 6, 8 and 10)
The house was designed by architect Josef Chochol and built in 1912 – 1913. It has a saddle roof and mansard windows. The gable of the central house contains a sculpture with a scene from Czech mythology. Josef Chochol also designed other Cubist houses below Vyšehrad. Not far from the triple family house there is a villa with a garden in Libušina Street and another on the corner of Neklanova Street No. 30.

Mánes and the Šítkov Water Tower (Prague 2 – Nové Město, Masarykovo nábřeží 250)
The plans for this functionalist building came from architect Otakar Novotný, and he designed it for the Society of Artists named after Mánes. It was built in 1928 – 1930. The exhibition halls, café and restaurant are favourite meeting places not only for artists but for all art-lovers.
The Mánes building stands on the site of the former Šítkov mills, nov recalled only by the old water tower, the first mention of which dates from 1495.

The Building of the Nationale Nederlanden on the Rašín Embankment, which the people of Prague call "The Dancing House" or "Ginger and Fred". (Prague 2 – Nové Město, Rašínovo nábřeží No. 80)
This house, designed by architects V. Milunič and F. O. Gehry and built in 1994 – 1996, stands on one of the best sites in Prague with a view of the panorama of Hradčany. The facade giving onto Jirásek square is dominated by the left glass tower, recalling a gracefully flexed dancer – Ginger – and the right concrete tower with a metal cupola crowning it – Fred. The cupola constructed of metal tubes covered in a network of stainless metal sheet represents the head of Medusa and it was designed by architect F. O. Gehry.

PRAGUE
A PHOTOGRAPHIC GUIDE TO PRAGUE
– LATEST, ENLARGED EDITION
Photographs: © Jiří Šourek
Concept and text: © Hana Bílková
Translation: Norah Hronková
Published by the Artfoto Publishers, Štupartská 7, 110 00 Prague 1
tel. 224 826 906, tel., fax: 224 826 905
www.artfoto-prague.cz
as their 49th publication
Editor: Hana Bílková
1st edition
© Artfoto Praha
Repro and print: Tiskárny B.N.B. Velké Poříčí

ISBN 80-86085-39-2